AF411961

Simon Periton

Simon Periton

Sadie Coles HQ, London   Koenig Books, London

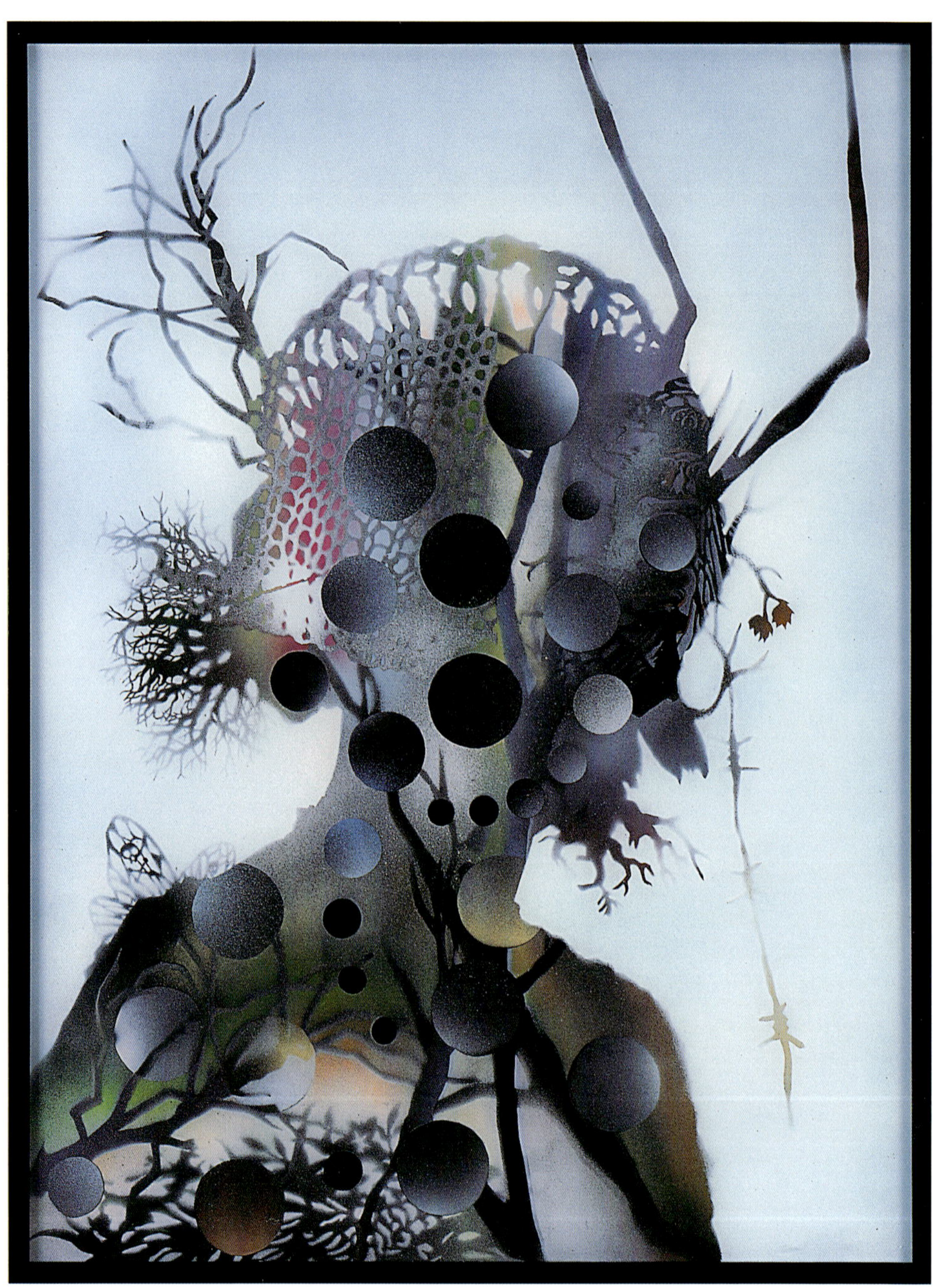

The Poacher, 2007, 82 × 62 cm, spray paint on glass

Into the Shadowland: Ultra-Vivid Ornamentalism

Michael Bracewell
on the work of Simon Periton

The honey-bags steal from the humble bees,
And for night-tapers crop their waxen thighs,
And light them at the fiery glow-worm's eyes
Shakespeare, *A Midsummer Night's Dream*, Act III Scene I

The patterning of the background is softened and diaphanous; complex, maddening near tessellations of shape and form are revealed in negative outline, their busy undergrowth of imagery rendered slick and exuberant by sharply contrasting tones of pale pastel and sickly fluorescence. It is a dense, cloying association of colour and detail – at once synthetic, chemical and redolent of enchantment. Swarming in disarray, yet stilled, as though they had left the imprint of their clamour on the palest of early morning mist, fronds and petals, briar stems, mesh and meandering chains appear to present the ghosts of themselves in the colours of long forgotten confectionery: apple and blueberry and mandarin sherbet, dusted with liquorice.

Against this bewitching mass of somewhat queasy colour, there is the silhouette of what appears to be an advancing female figure, dressed in a costume of archaic, regal design, and wearing a crown of antennae-like horns. Her right arm ends with a protrusile, deadly-looking knife – a prosthetic hand and forearm comprising a scalpel blade to human scale, ideally weighted to stabbing and cutting. Her left arm is bent, daintily, and raised upwards at the elbow, lending her entire demeanour a doubly courtly attitude.

What holds the viewer's gaze in this dramatic image – a painting on glass made by Simon Periton, and called, with somewhat sinister resonance, *The Governess* (2007) – is the forceful confluence of effects through which the portentous sentience of the ghostly figure becomes animated against the lighter colours and finer shapes from which it seems to emerge. In addition to which, this is a figure that appears robotic, mechanical and futuristic, yet also drawn from the pageantry of fairy tales, or a modern romantic reclamation of ornate medievalism. Threat, menace and inscrutability are its defining characteristics – Titania as Mrs Scissorhands, perhaps, or the Bride of Terminator – just as intoxicating sweetness and fabular mystery seem to exude from the background.

Between the middle years of the 1990s and the opening years of the twenty-first century, Periton made a succession of iconic works in the determinedly anachronistic medium of the paper doily – the quaintness of the chosen form pop-culturally usurped and expanded to epic proportions. The collision in these pieces between exquisitude of craft and aggression of subject matter could be seen within a lineage of English wit, from the diabolist Orientalism of Aubrey Beardsley's late nineteenth-century illustrations to *Salome* (1894) and *The Rape of The Lock* (1896) (for example), through to such artefacts as the muslin shirts made by Vivienne Westwood and Malcolm McLaren for their punk boutique Seditionaries.

It is a methodology in which the role of irony is crucial. The appropriation of delicacy – of that which is translucent, genteel, modest, seemly – to be the bearer of confrontational signage, is an act of knowing and intentional ambiguity. The gravitational field of cultural status is turned upside down – that which was rebellious becomes domestic, and that which was conservative acquires enhanced radicalism. Likewise, games are played with materiality and narrative, in which the accepted qualities of each are both reversed and intensified. Prettiness and violence become reflections of one another; the delicate tracery of finely wrought craft makes eloquent brutality and coarseness.

In these earlier works, made by the cutting of fine materials to create silhouettes and patterns of extravagant, often wittily aggressive design, Periton pioneered an aesthetic which subscribed in part to the simultaneous exuberance and inscrutability of Pop art, and in part to the glancing Mock Heroism that can be seen as the armed wing, so to speak, of modern Camp. Yet there is an intensity of purpose to the epic scope of these 'doily' and cut pieces that transposes their articulation of form and colour into declamatory statements – as beguiling and aesthetically luxurious as they were oppositional and determinedly insular. Smashed walls, winged insects,

Agri-Culture 2 (detail), 2004, 157 × 206 cm, coloured papers, two layers

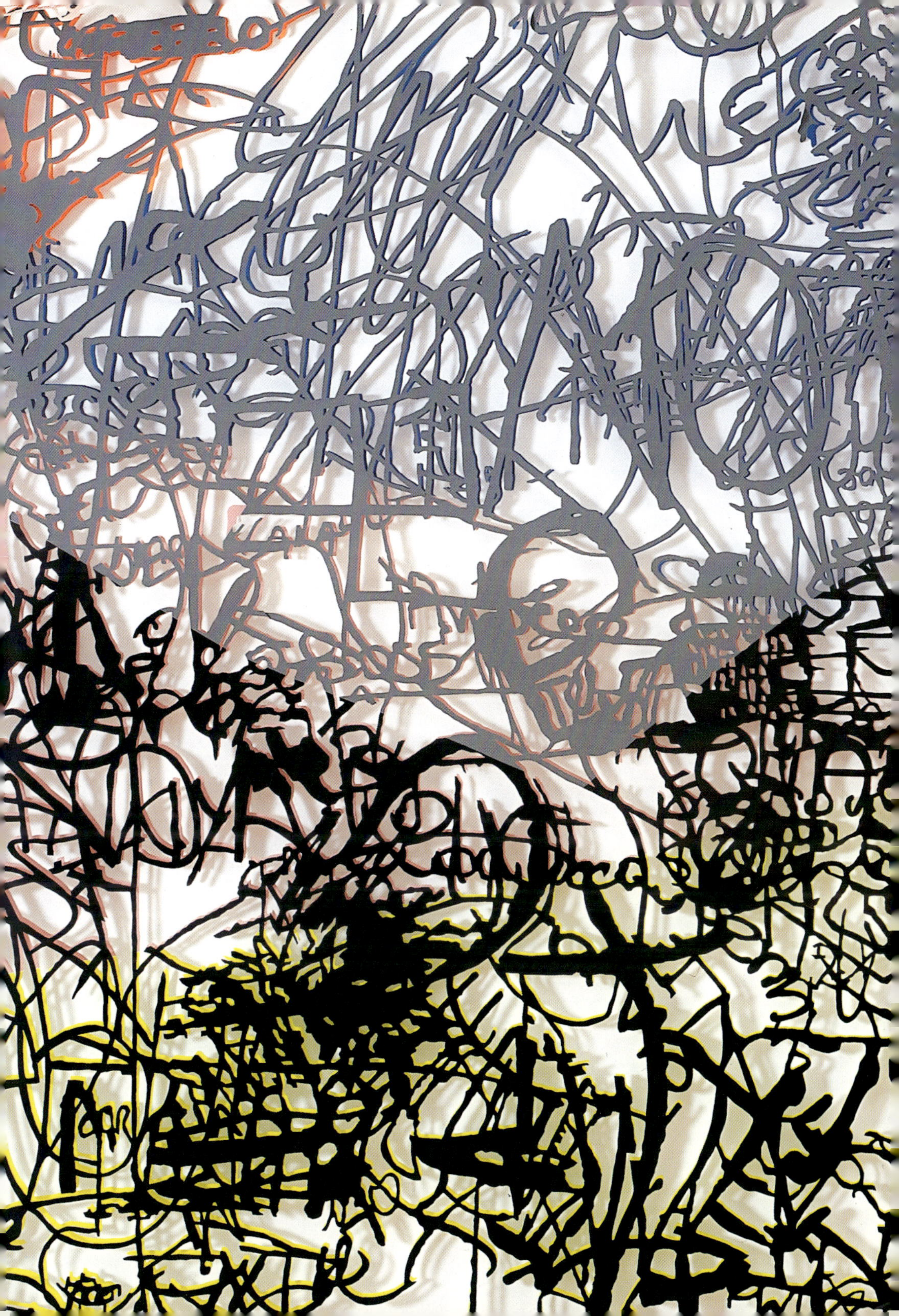

the staring mask of American punk icon Iggy Pop, grotesque, cartoon-like patternings of explosive farts and anarchy symbols; in his articulation of such subjects through a medium of seemingly genteel delicacy (the viewer might be reminded of Regency silhouettes and ornamentation, the design of high Victorian ceramics or the dark confabulations of the German Gothic), Periton created works which re-wired both the art-making process and cultural expectation. These were Pop-hip reclamations of the aphoristic languor of Aesthetic Movement chic; works which were Dandified in their philosophical games with style and meaning, yet dense with subcultural critique.

As important, however, is the way in which these 'doily' works can be seen to have opened the vision of Periton's art-making. In material terms, the 'cut-out' pieces all made use of a particular engagement with light, weight and transparency. In both their visual and their tactile qualities, these were works which appeared to occupy space in a manner at once web-like, ceremonial and sentient; the narrative drama of their subject matter was revealed by what had been cut away, as was the drama of their form. The intense visual impact of the work was thus created by a tension between absence and presence, enchanted meaning and pictorial void.

Favouring either black, or softer, brighter, pastel shades, these 'doily' pieces made a creative virtue of their varied internal contradictions to establish both a palette and a sensibility. Their mood is at once seductive, humorous, detached, menacing, inscrutable and violent. In his subsequent paintings on glass, however, Periton advances and consolidates all of these qualities, pioneering strange new worlds of intellectual imagination, and uncovering a shadowland of twilit romanticism, perverse allegory and heightened form.

●

In both process and content, the art of Simon Periton has always stood independently of any prevailing trend or school of art-making. In his paintings on glass, Periton maintains this steady position, creating a succession of works which appear to describe their own pervasive mood of aesthetic enchantment and lowering portent. If *The Governess* gives some indication of the tense, ambiguous and highly atmospheric territory that is occupied

Smilie Rag, 2004, 132 × 121.9 cm, fluorescent pink, beige, pale blue paper

by these paintings, then *Hop Picker* (2007) – in which we see what appear to be the head and shoulders of a skeletal robot sentinel, its head encircled in curlicues of baroque ironwork and barbed wire – gives further evidence of their pictorial tone. *Stealer* (2007) and *Back to Nature* (2007), are denser in detail and of darker colour – they have a nocturnal, woodland feel to them – but the imagistic continuity is constant.

In simple mechanical terms, Periton makes these works by creating masks and templates of patterning material on the back of a sheet of glass, and then spraying the successive layers with ordinary car paints. Crucially, much of the material which is laid upon the glass to create the resulting image is discarded, left-over, remnants and fragments which have accumulated in Periton's studio – material thus making the alchemical transition from being unwanted dross, to bearer of form and meaning. The painting is then revealed on the reverse side of the glass, its form dictated by the resulting shapes and silhouettes created by the paint spray across the templates.

As can be seen in the intimations of silvery moonlit flora and fauna in *Bank Holiday Monday* (2007) or the Dulacesque blue reverie of *Stealer*, the dexterity with which Periton assembles and deploys this art-making process can achieve results, in terms of painting, of profound pictorial depth and imagistic intensity. One might be in some mutant, art historical time tunnel, through which the psychedelic arts of the latter half of the 1960s are merged with the fantastical temperament of British neo-Romanticism of the mid-1930s to mid-1950s. As regards the former, Simon Reynolds has usefully summarised the territory in his essay, *Love or Confusion: Psychedelic Rock in the Sixties* (2005). His description of the artistic DNA of psychedelic music and styling might be applied point for point to the heady and conflicting imagistic constitution of Periton's paintings on glass:

'On the one hand, it was totally modern, an art form based on amplification technology and sheer inundating volume of sound, on the aesthetic possibilities of electricity (from effects such as feedback to the lightshows that backdropped psychedelic bands). Yet in the lyrics, the folk-derived vocals and the presence of acoustic instruments, you could detect an equally strong impulse to reject modernity and the city, a longing to go back to nature. Psychedelic songs teemed with imagery of the rustic and rootsy, while clothing and album artwork alluded to frontier America, Edwardian England and medieval Europe.'

The magic ingredient, so to speak, in what Reynolds terms the 'ultra-vivid ornamentalism' of psychedelia, is of course the eerie, supernatural world of Victorian and Edwardian faery tale illustration – itself more than lightly tethered to the diabolistic fantasies of French and British symbolism of the period between 1860 and 1900. And as though to cement the psychedelia of the High Sixties to the dream worlds of late Victoriana, Reynolds subsequently quotes a lyric by Dorothy Moskowitz, from the 1968 self-titled album by softly experimental psychedelic rockers, The United States of America:

Poisonous gardens, lethal and sweet
Venomous blossoms, choleric fruit deadly to eat
Violet nightshades, innocent bloom,
Omnivorous orchids, cautiously wait, hungrily loom
You will find them in her eyes, in her eyes, in her eyes.

The imagery in Periton's paintings on glass includes many of the components one might recognise from the faery and fantasy illustrations by, for instance, Edmund Dulac, Arthur Rackham or Edward Detmold: monarchs, foliage, wings, petals, chains, mesh, briar, seed pods, a hooded figure, spindle-like twigs or spider legs. From such ingredients one might imagine summoning the supernatural realms as depicted by Daisy Makeig – Jones (1881–1945) in her line of 'Fairyland Lustre' designs for bone china. As Rodney Engen conveys the scene from the 'Ghostly Wood (Nursery Fairies)' ceramic, based upon a folk tale from *The Legends of Croquemitaine* (1863): "…a journey through the fearsome 'Land of Illusion', peopled by lost souls, demon trees and ghastly apparitions, to conquer the 'Fortress of Fear'…"

We might easily be within the fantastical acid landscape described by Dorothy Moskowitz (or any number of psychedelic lyricists) – but the subjects of Periton's paintings on glass take the visionary ambience of such specifically gothic fantasy as more of a departure point than an imagined destination. For it is the element of detritus and discard in Periton's art-making process, and the haphazard discourse that it established between considered authorship on the one hand, and chance, generative creativity on the other,

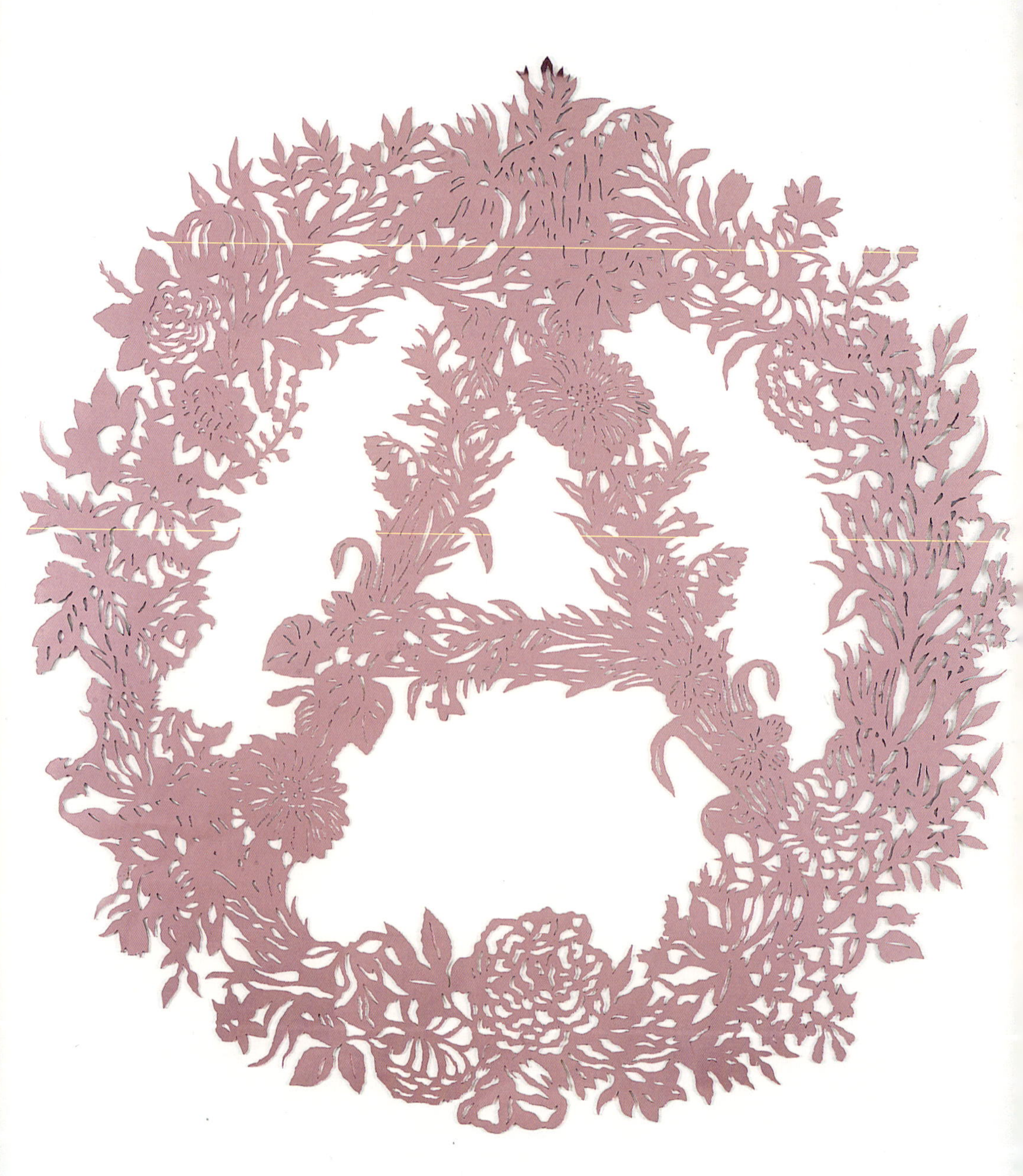

which shifts both the form and the mood of these paintings on glass into an impressionistic terrain which maintains close links to science fiction, post-industrialism and a kind of hybrid Baroque-Surrealist Futurism. The pictorial results being as though apocalyptic morality tales such as the science fiction feature films *Blade Runner* (1982) or *The Terminator* (1984) had been conceived and styled in the spirit of psychedelia's reclamation of faery symbolism.

In such a dizzying maze of styles and influences, therefore, born of the outline of waste materials, one might locate an allegory: that here is a shadowland of contemporary cultural detritus – a faery world of exile, misfit and awkwardness, in which that which has been rejected from the suave, smoothed society of modern image-making pursues its own ghostly rites, as free of logic and reason as it is from formal aesthetics or critical theory. To make a further, and in this context somewhat ironic, comparative allusion – the 'world' described by these paintings on glass is a Never-Never-Land of ghosts and shadows and wreckage, its air, seemingly, an hallucinogen to tourists.

●

In *New Dawn Fades* (2007), we are faced with a scene that might be taken from one of the artist, film-maker and writer Derek Jarman's (1942–1994) cinematic fantasies of post-punk London. As Jarman made an imagistic fetish of royalty, and of the corruptibility – as much as the pageantry – of sovereign power, so the crowned monarch who takes her place in *New Dawn Fades* is seen in black silhouette, and to a seemingly broiling background of orange mist and dark clouds.

As depicted by Periton, the seated royal figure is fenced off by what seem to be broad, taut crossings of barbed wire, a tangle of thorns at their base. There are also strands of viciously mean barbed wire to the lower right of the painting, and silhouettes of what might be dying weeds, with spiked seed pods. Between the Queen's shoulder blades we see translucent butterfly wings, and before her – dropping from the lower clouds like some Biblical phenomena – the flaring outline of what might be dried flora, but what appears like forked lightening. The effect is heroic and imperial – patriotic even, as though the image were captured during the *blitzkrieg* air attacks

Addi, 2006, 100 cm (diameter), mirrored perspex

on London. For Periton, who has previously worked with punk imagery in pieces such *as S.P.* (1995) or *The Damned* (2001), the iconic resonance of Jamie Reid's usurpation of Cecil Beaton's portrait of Queen Elizabeth II would also be a significant cultural reference point, and can be found in his paintings *The Poacher* (2007), *The Operator* (2007) and *The Gamekeeper* (2007).

All of these paintings comprise notions of Englishness and sovereignty, with intimations of disaster, war, history and the co-existence of natural and supernatural worlds. As such, it is a form of art-making which might have descended in spirit from the neo-Romantic period in British art – identified by David Alan Mellor as occurring between 1935 and 1955 – to reincarnate as commemorative of English punk's dystopic vision of the future. The paintings of such neo-Romantic British artists as John Craxton, Leslie Hurry and particularly Graham Sutherland, share a darkling, portentous and at times terrifying view of what Mellor so elegantly described, in his essay on Hurry, *Towards the Nuclear Future* (1987), as "obscured places where curses of history and hysteria spoke together."

In the same essay, Mellor follows what might be a topography of influences on Periton's paintings on glass – works made in the same deep future, with poetic irony, that the neo-Romantic artists had discerned within their plangent, anxious, somnambulist reveries on a dying and buried England. "…a taste for detailed surface ornament" (wrote Raymond Mortimer for The New Statesman of Hurry's Redfern Gallery, London, show in December, 1941), "which we find in Anglo-Saxon illuminations, in Blake and nineteenth-century illustrations, such as Beardsley." Mellor then continues: "Spider webs of fragments floating on a thin surface plane, over jet-black depths, characterised Hurry's first large oil painting in this style…" The inheritance of such traits in Periton's paintings on glass is pronounced.

For these neo-Romantics, premonitions of apocalypse were identified in the sanctified and folkloric spaces of English culture. Serving as an art historical conduit between the spirit of neo-Romanticism and a 'No Future' vision of post-punk London, Derek Jarman would identify the end of England within a London re-imagined as a semi-derelict fascist state. In his film *The Last of England* (1987) imagery of hooded civil guards and desolate, fire-strewn wastelands frame the vision of refugees driven out of the ruins of their own

Schoolgirls, 2001, 81.5 × 61 cm, black, beige, crème paper

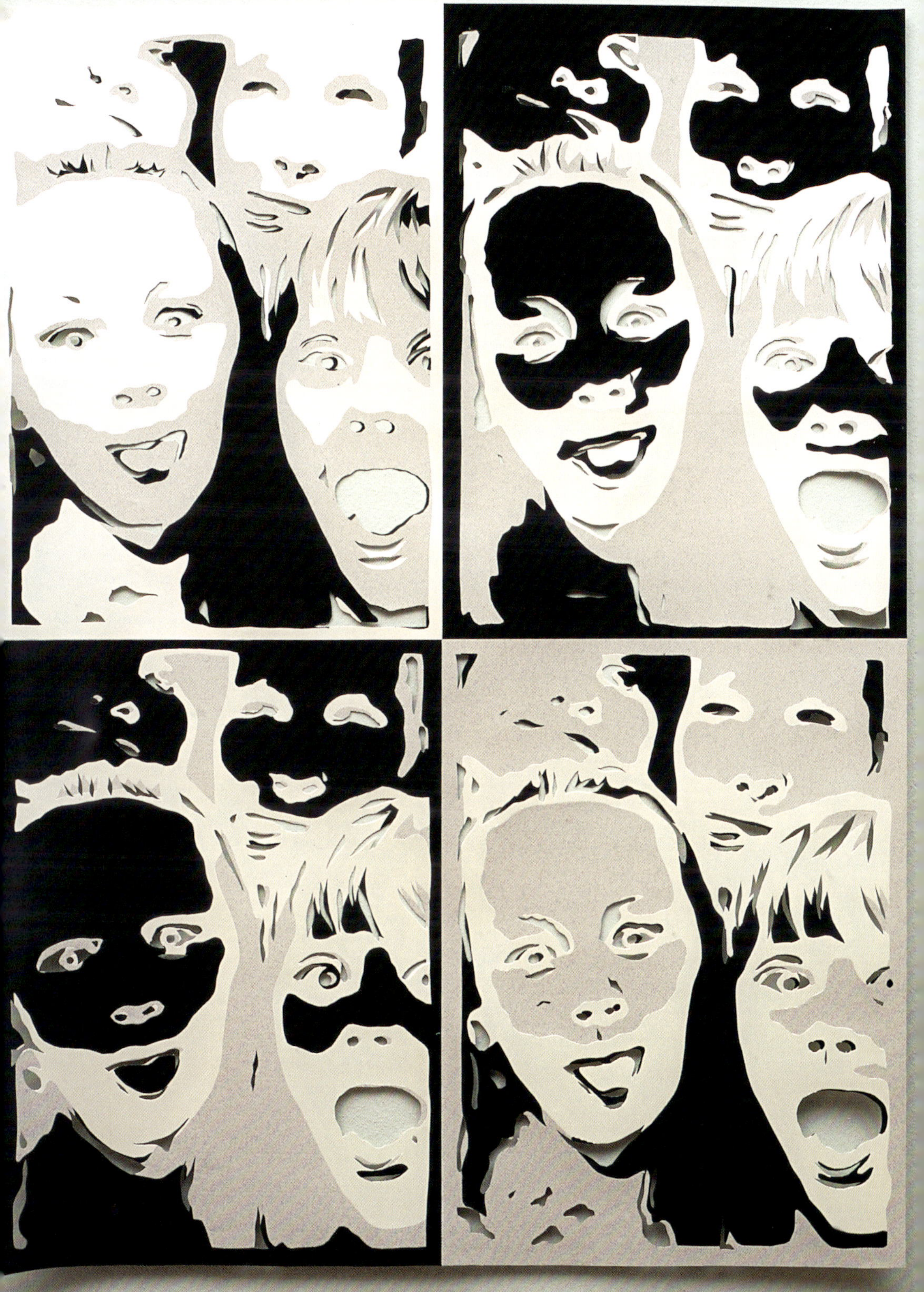

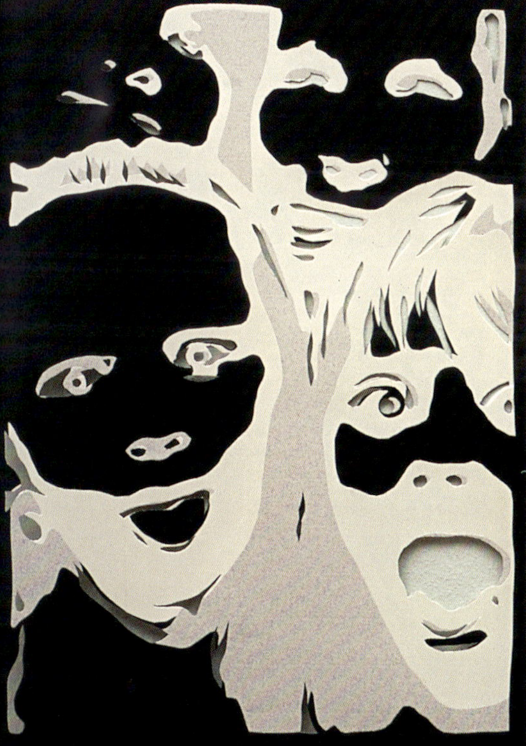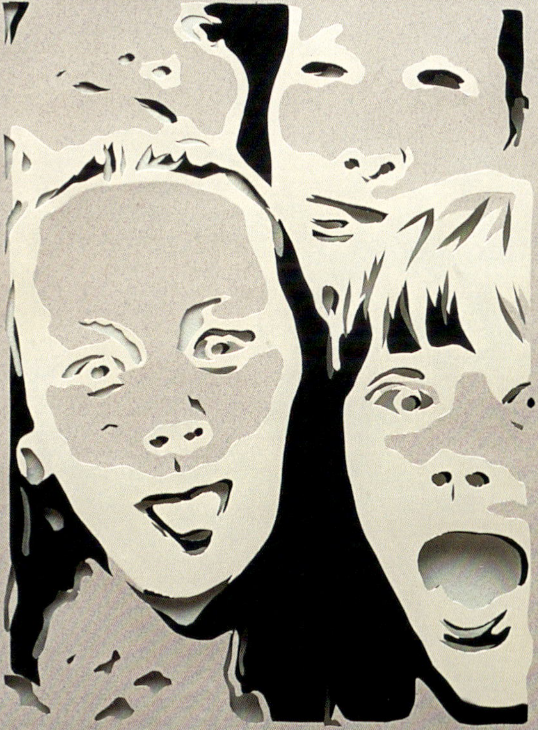

country. In the notes for this film, Jarman writes about the colour of his film: "The quality is something quite new, like stained glass, the film glows with wonderful colours. The video gives you a palette like a painter, and I find the result beautiful. The system produces blacks like the lead in stained glass, shadowy and mysterious, even when the sun is blazing. Much of *The Last of England* seems to be filmed at sundown, Eliot's violet hour."

Periton is an artist whose work is steeped in a particular, High Romantic notion of Englishness, and possesses the same ambivalent and ambiguous regard for landscape, craft, legend, pageantry and heroism (driven by a somewhat eighteenth-century sense of wit), that can be found in work as iconically British as the films of Michael Powell and Emeric Pressburger (themselves related to the tenets of neo-Romanticism) or the artisan culture of punk. In his tangerine edged enshrinement of Lawrence of Arabia (*Ghost Train* (2007)), for example, Periton thus luxuriates in the temper of improbable iconoclasts, and the charisma of their strange, somewhat otherworldly nobility. Likewise, the intensity of effect summoned up by Periton's paintings on glass is beguiling, contradictory, fantastical, eccentric, filled with presentiment and grotesquerie; a world comprised of its own heraldic past, and the shape of things to come.

Spaccanapoli 2 (detail), 2004, 165 × 215 cm, coloured papers, two layers

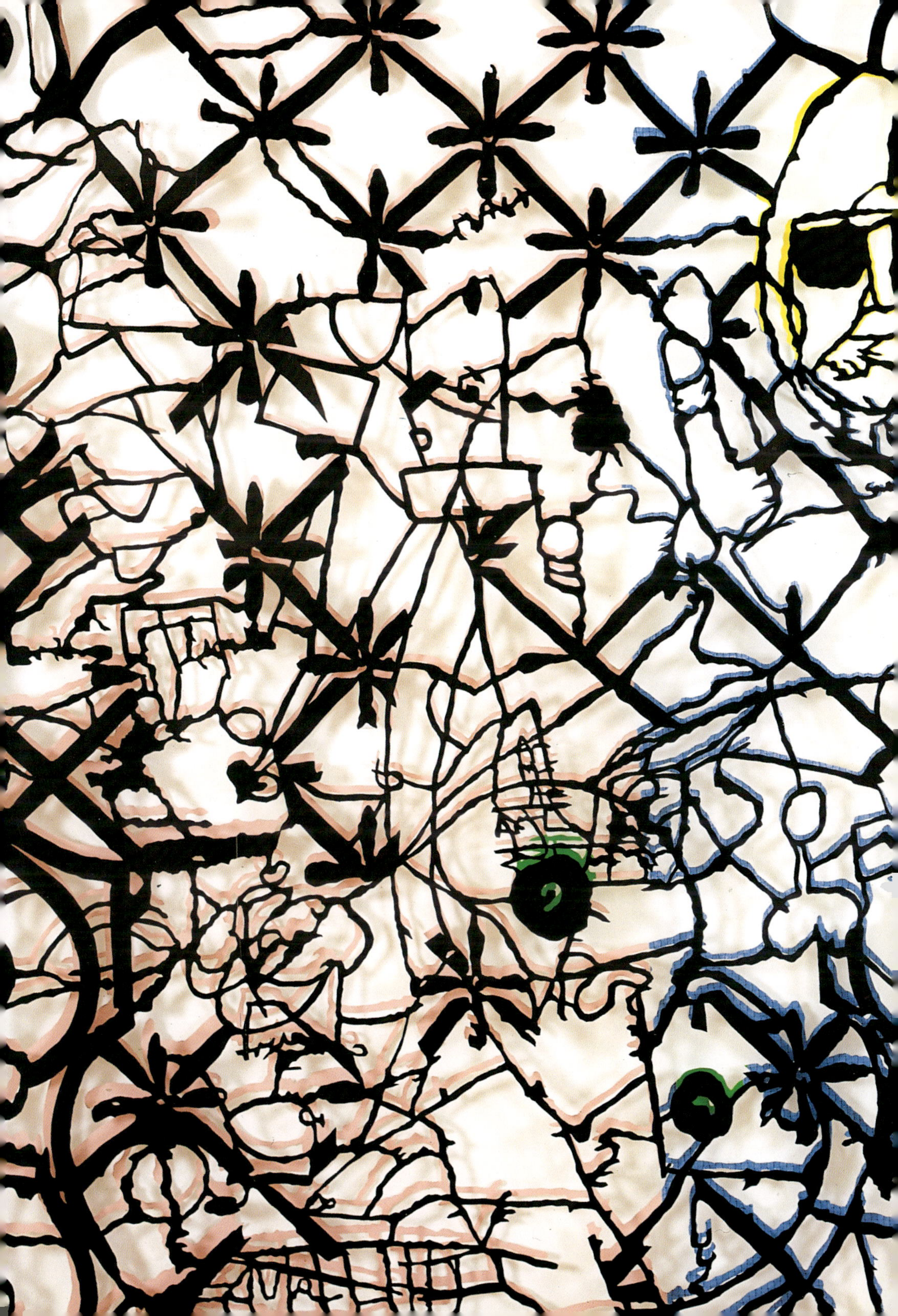

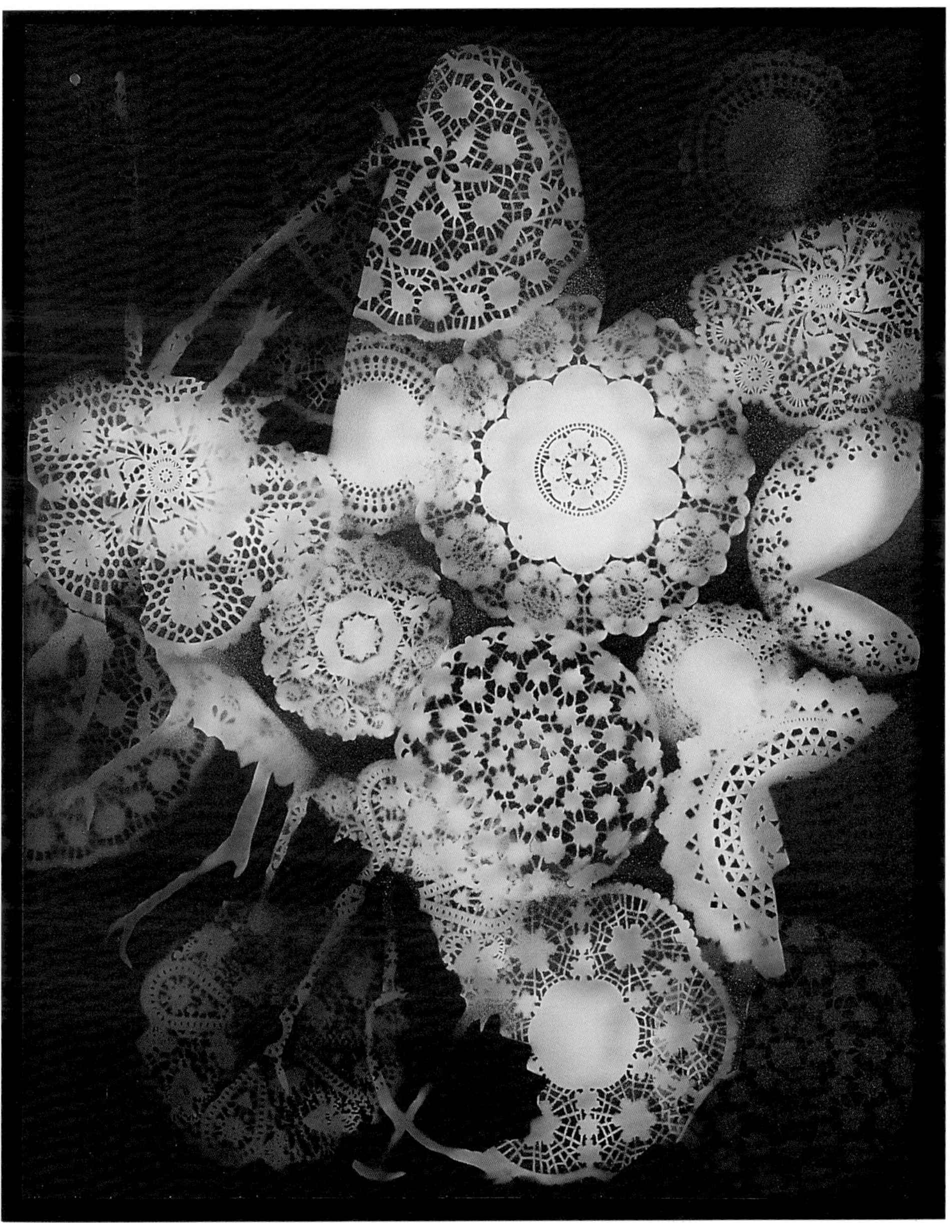

Solaris, 2006, 82 × 62 cm

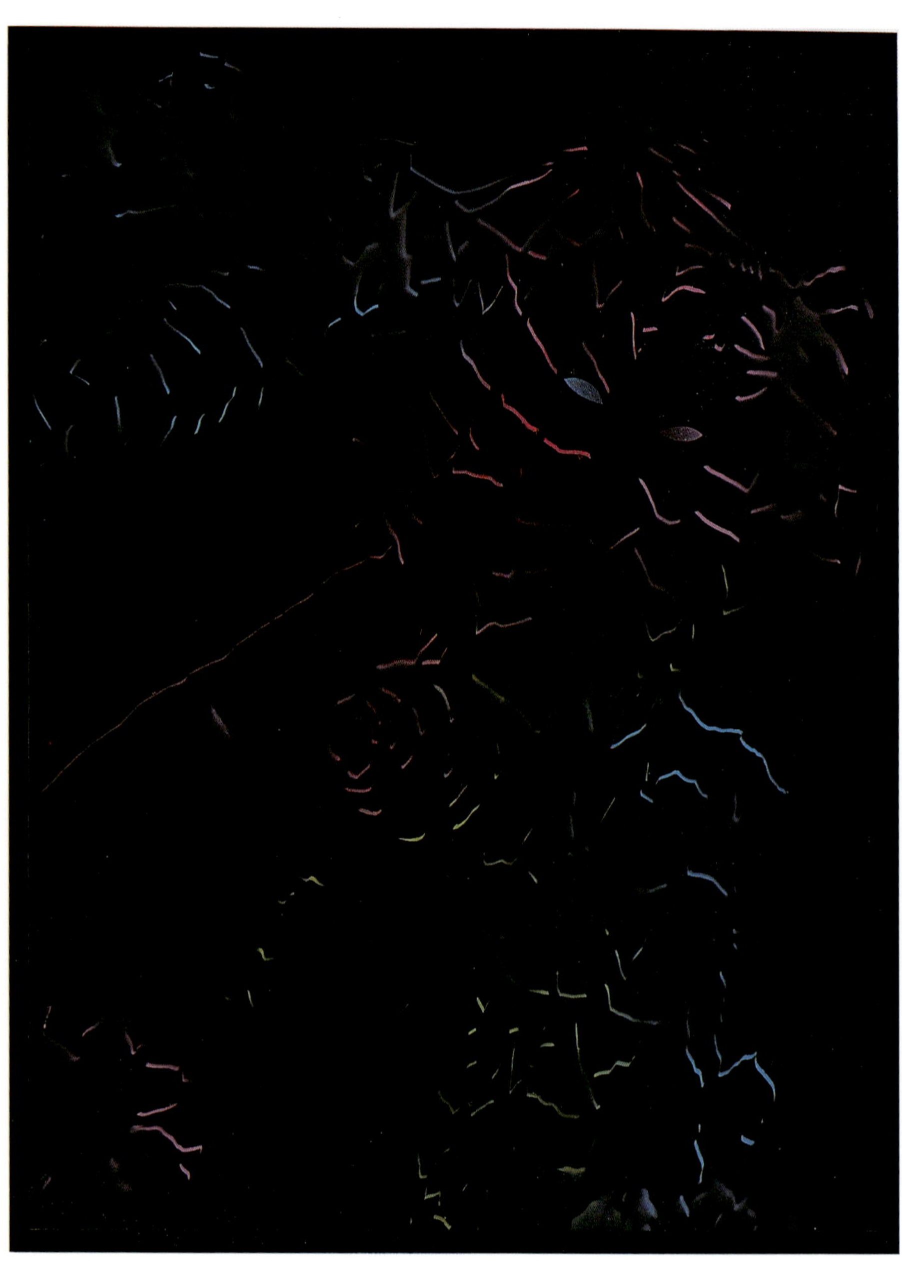

Avalanche, 2007, 82 × 62 cm

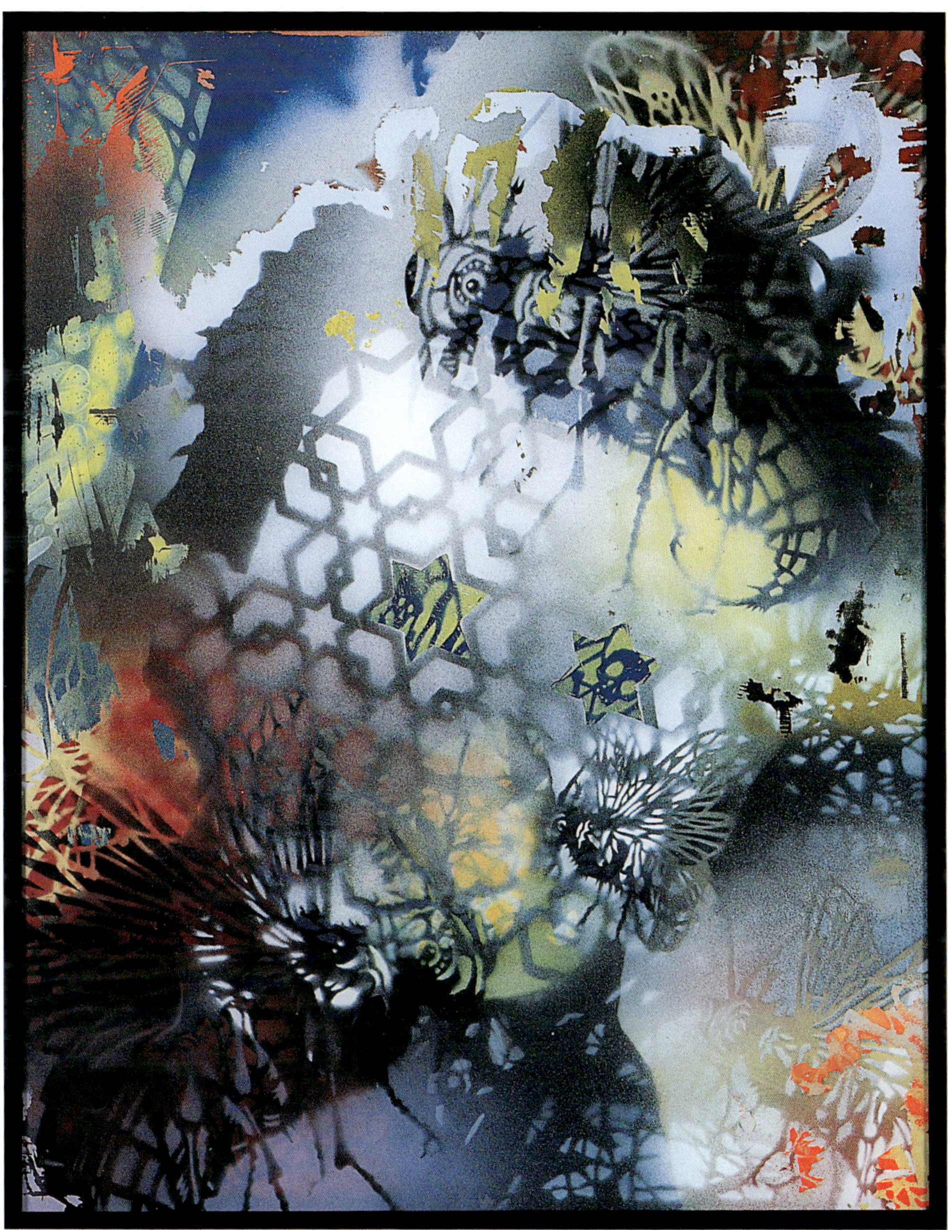

Ecstatic Cabaret, 2006, 52 × 41.7 cm

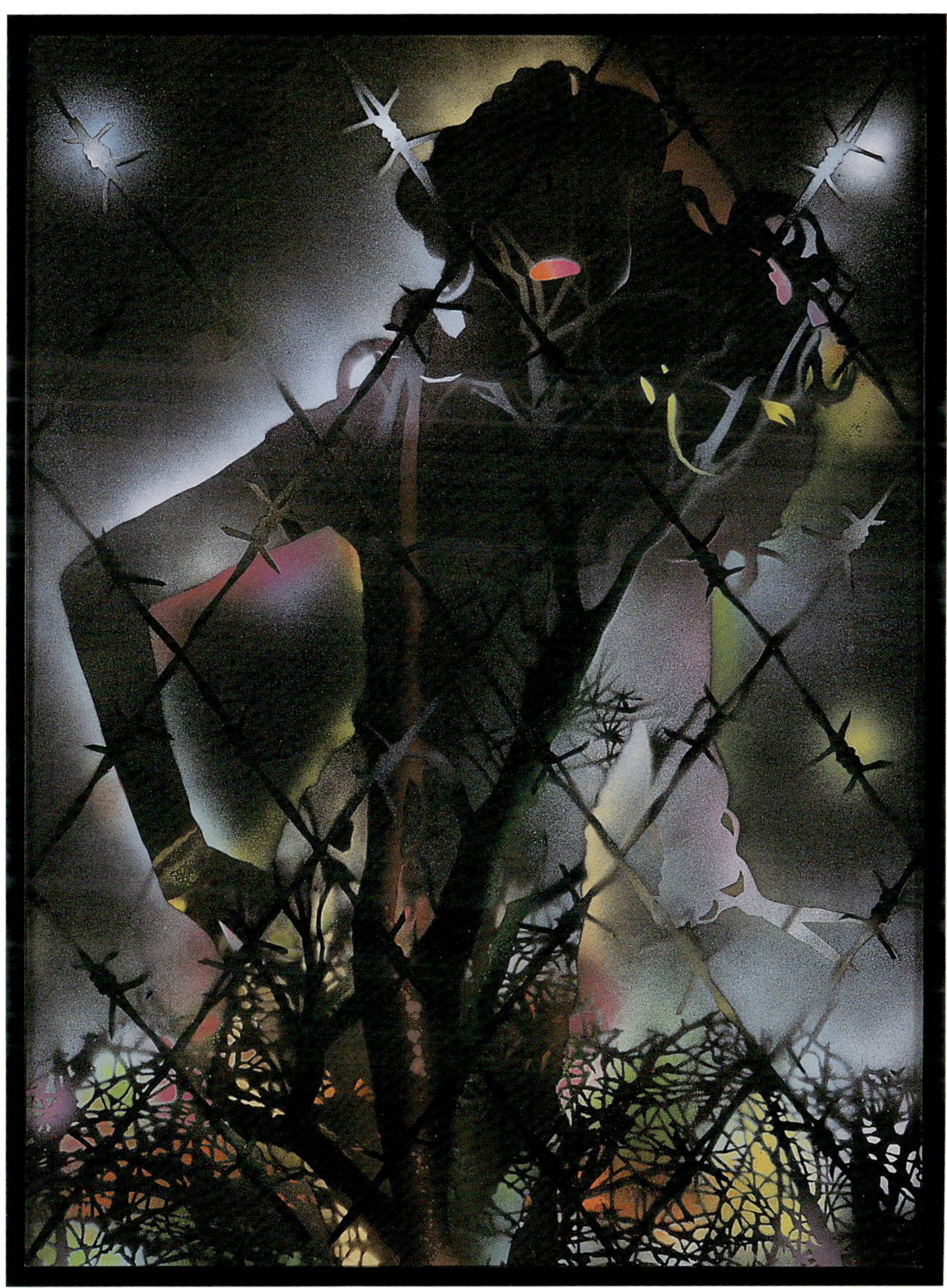

Unknown Pleasures, 2007, 82 × 62 cm

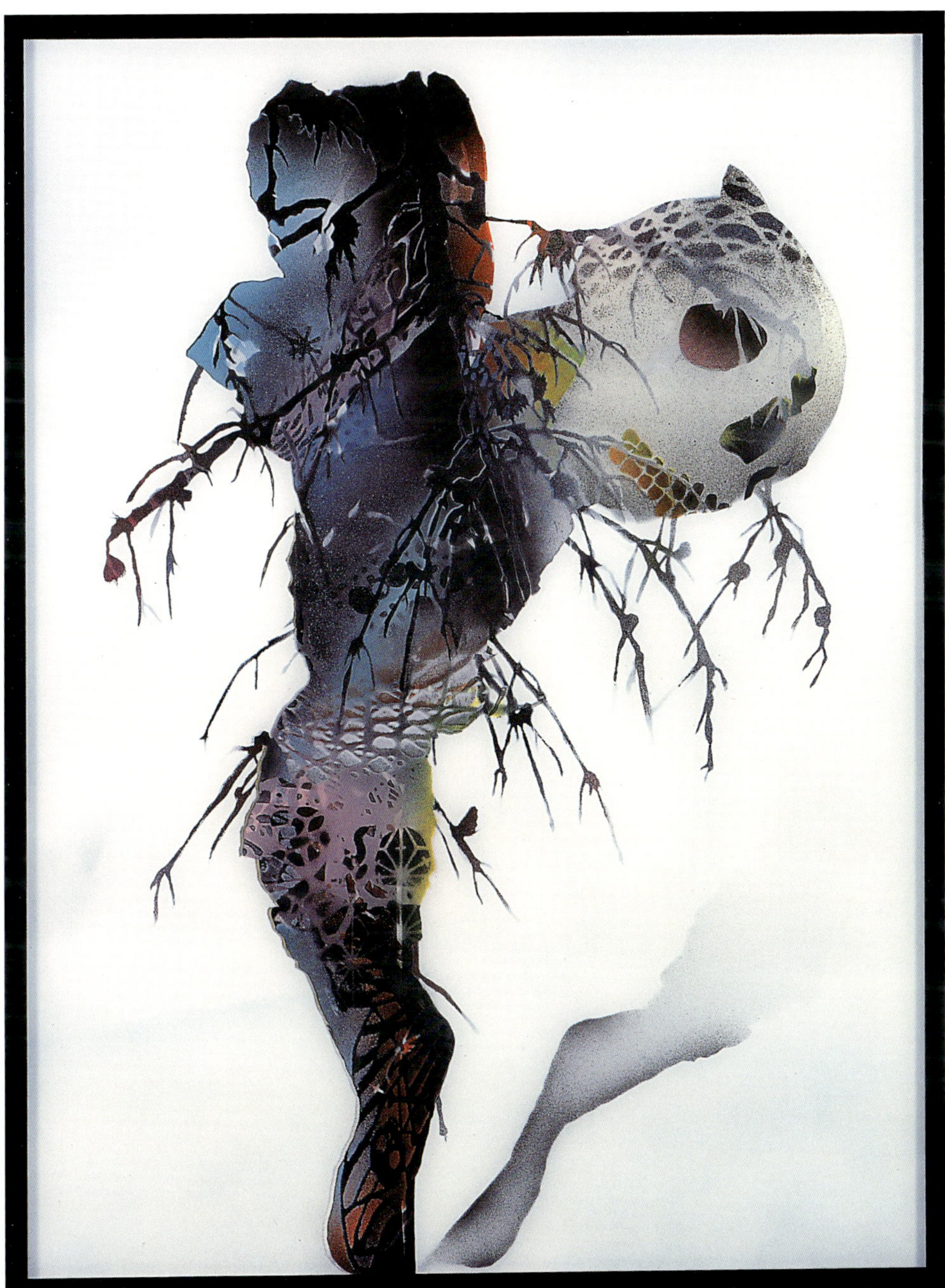

Natural Mystic, 2008, 82.5 × 62.5 cm

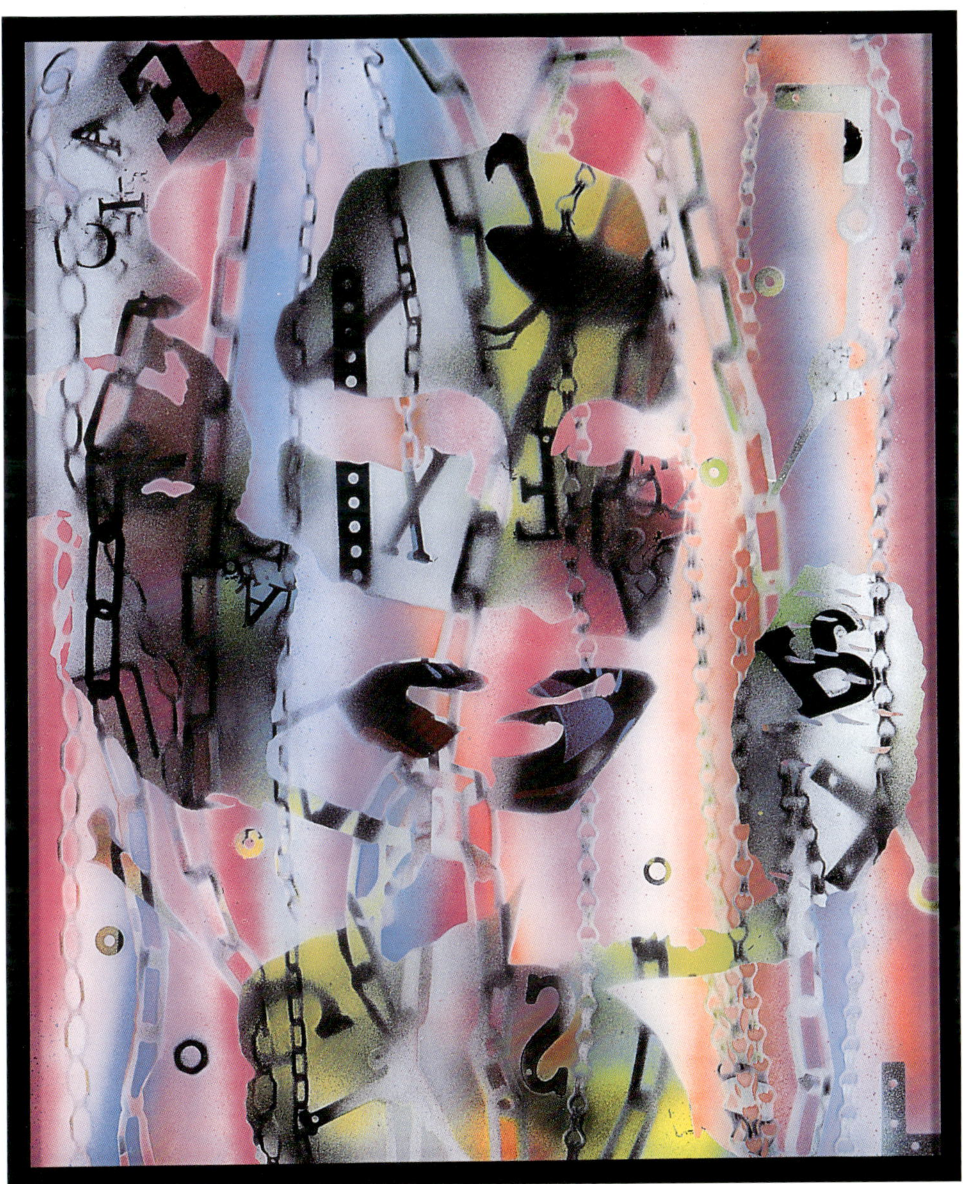

Brimstone, 2008, 61.8 × 51.8 cm

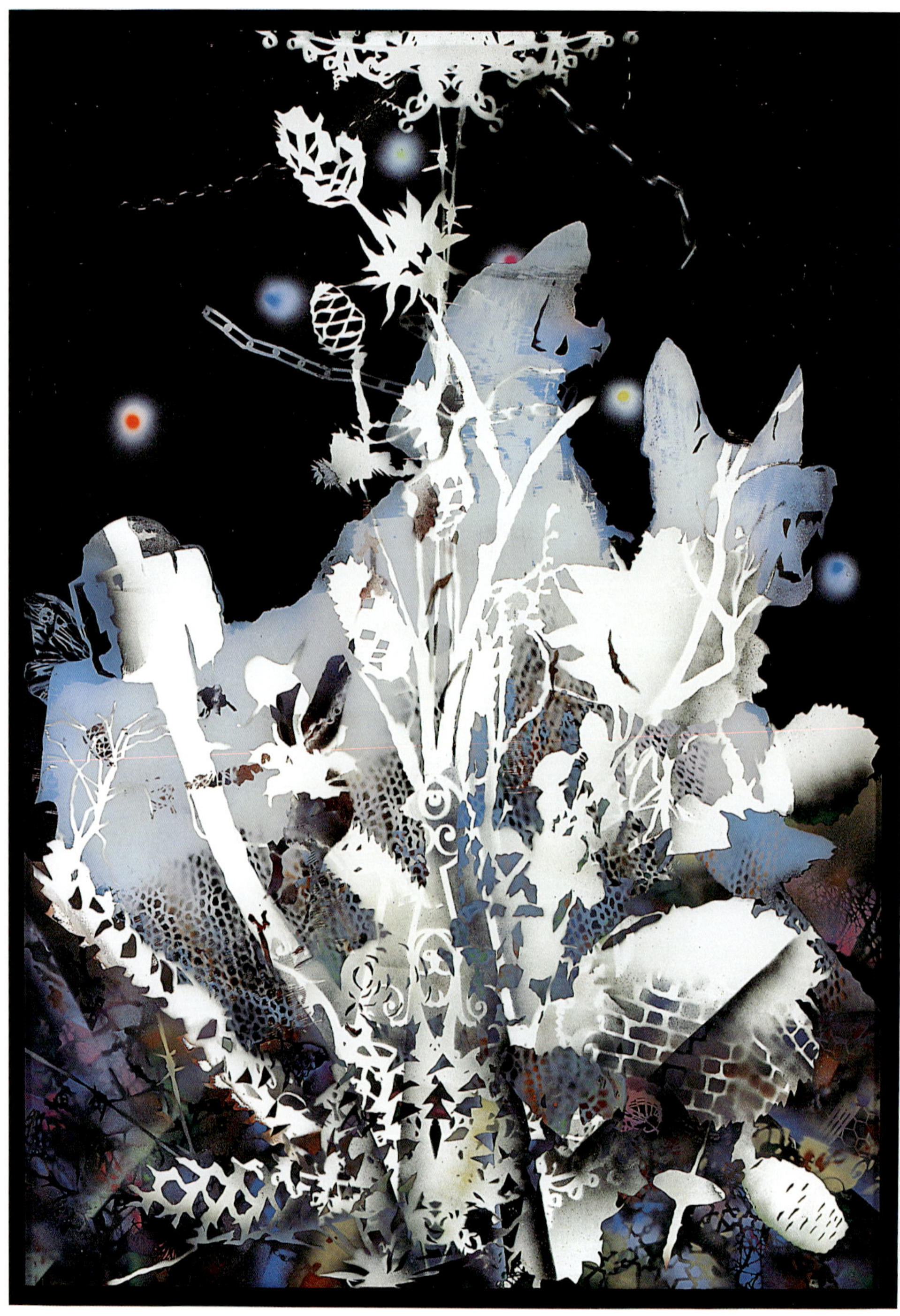

Bank Holiday Monday, 2007, 188.5 × 133.6 cm

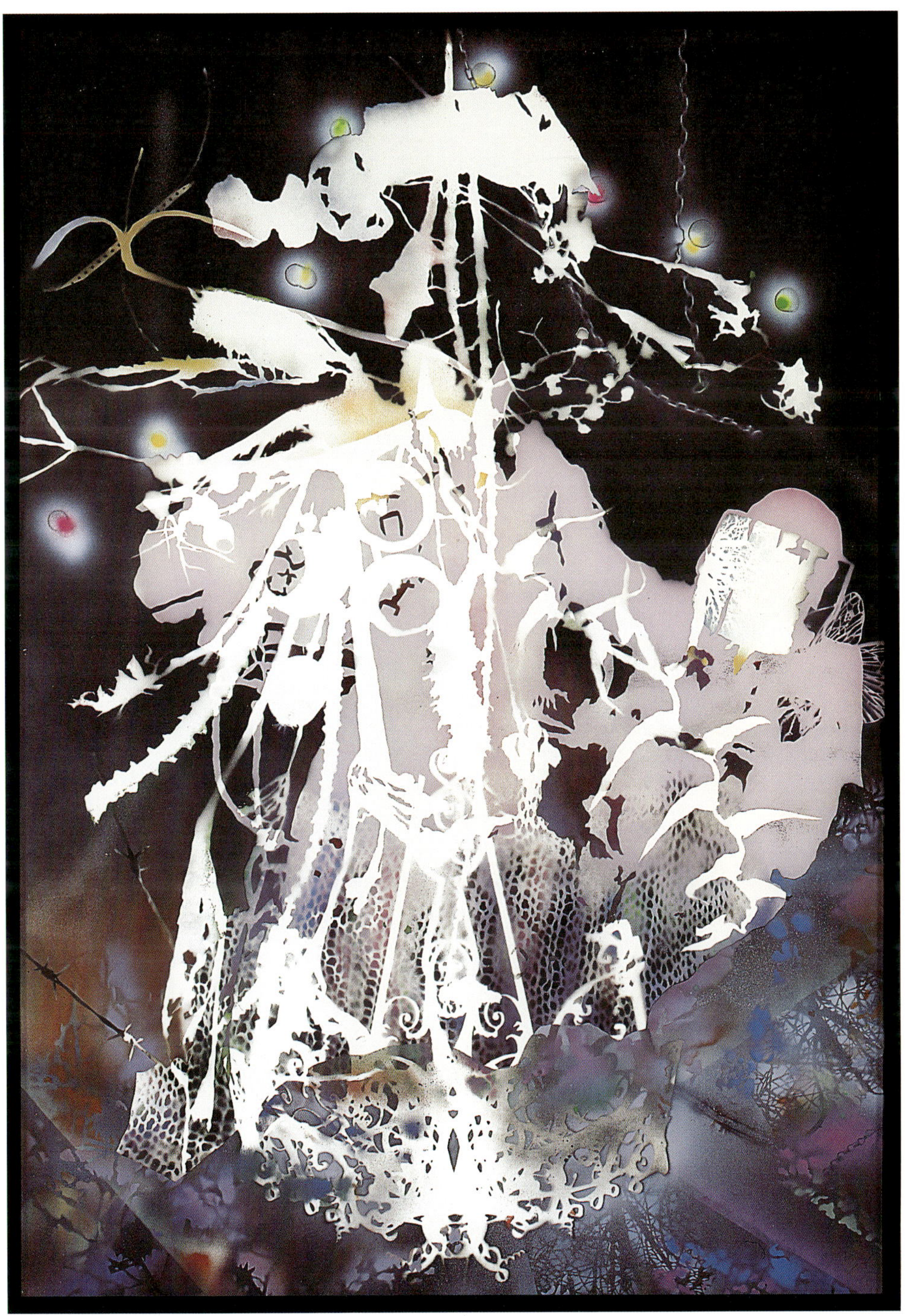

Waltzer, 2007, 188.5 × 133.6 cm

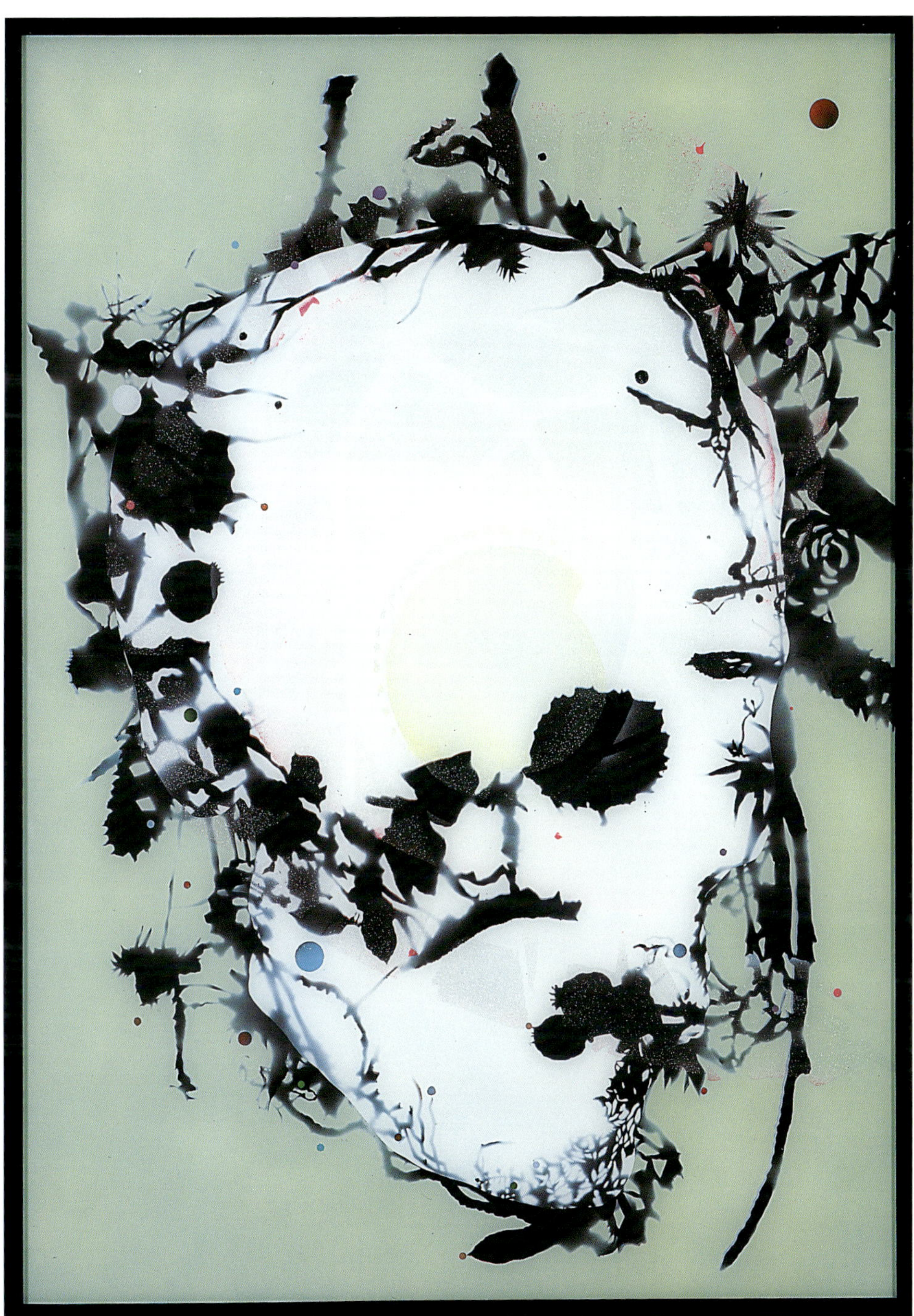

French Kiss, 2007, 163.5 × 118.50 cm

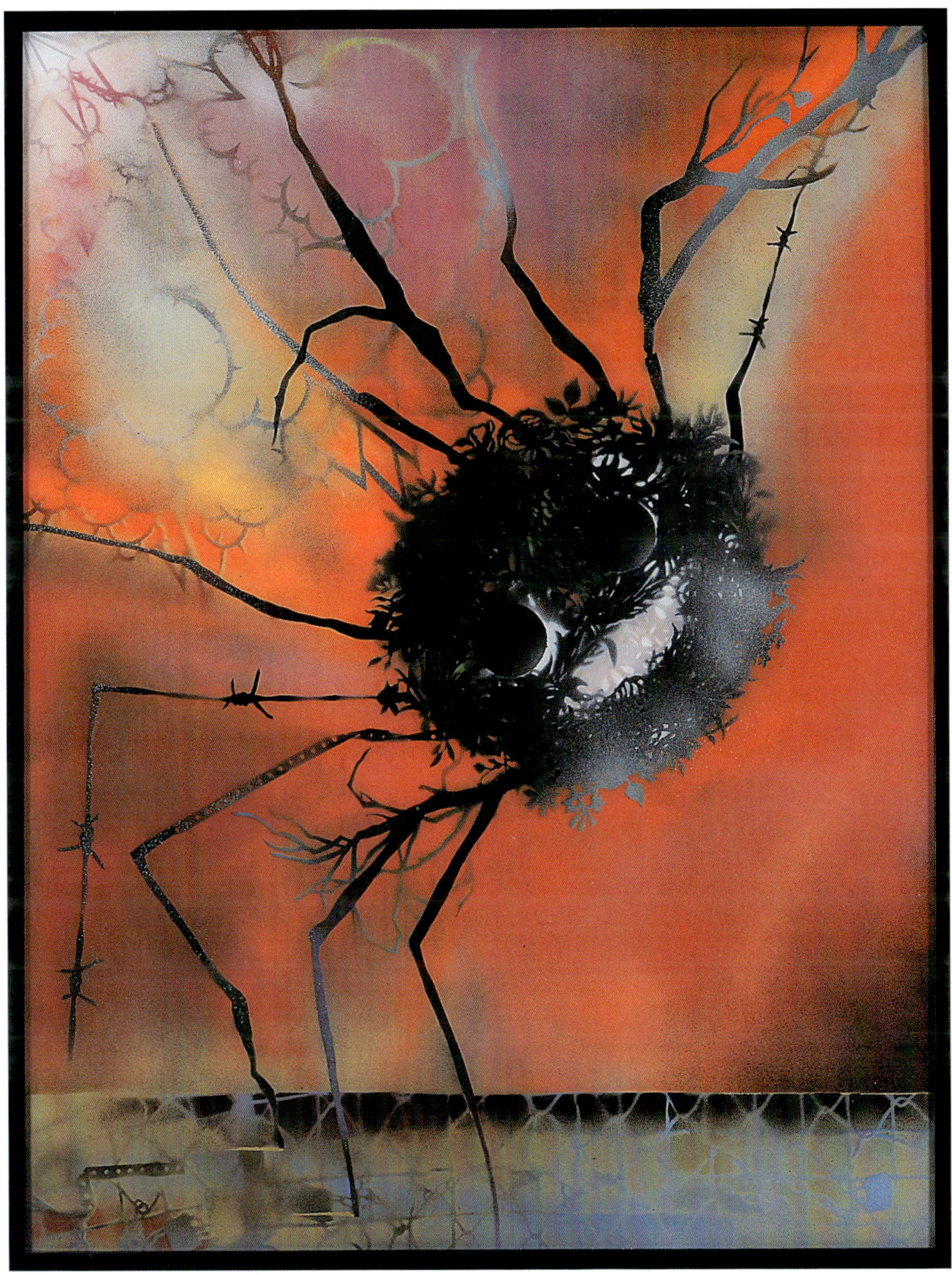

Day of the Lords, 2007, 128 × 99 cm

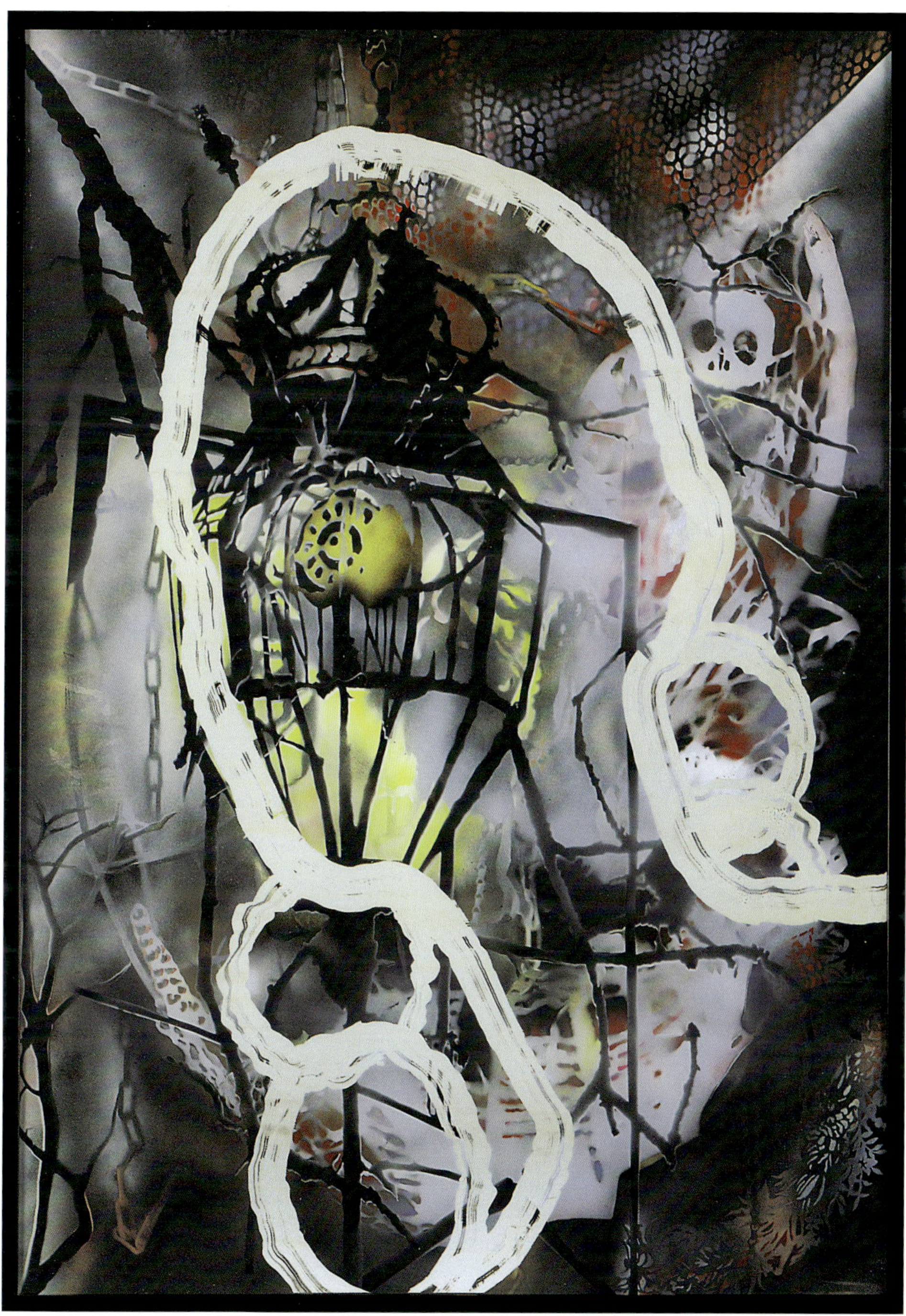

Countess, 2007, 163.5 × 118.5 cm

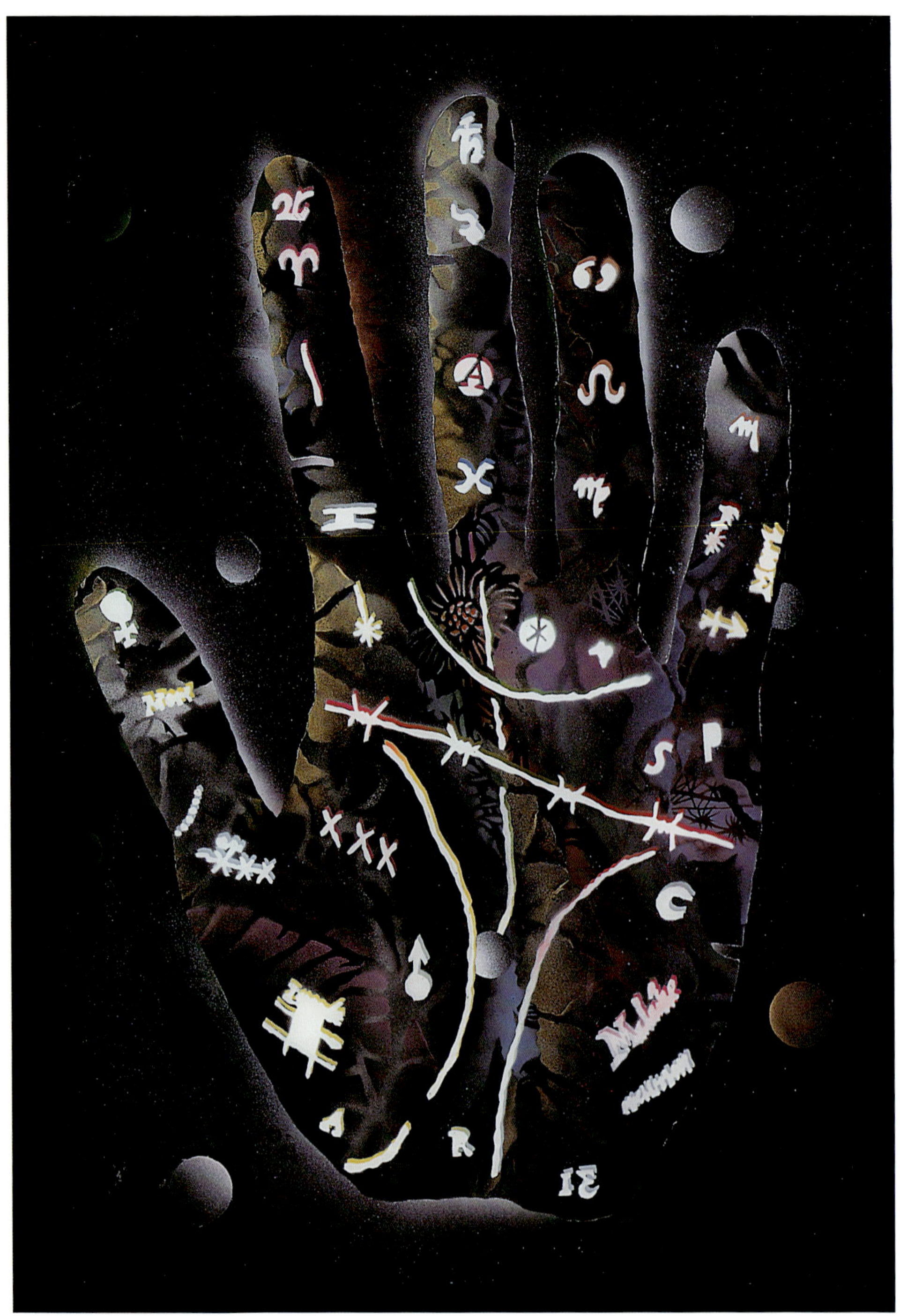

Premonitions (Dark), 2007, 103 × 73 cm

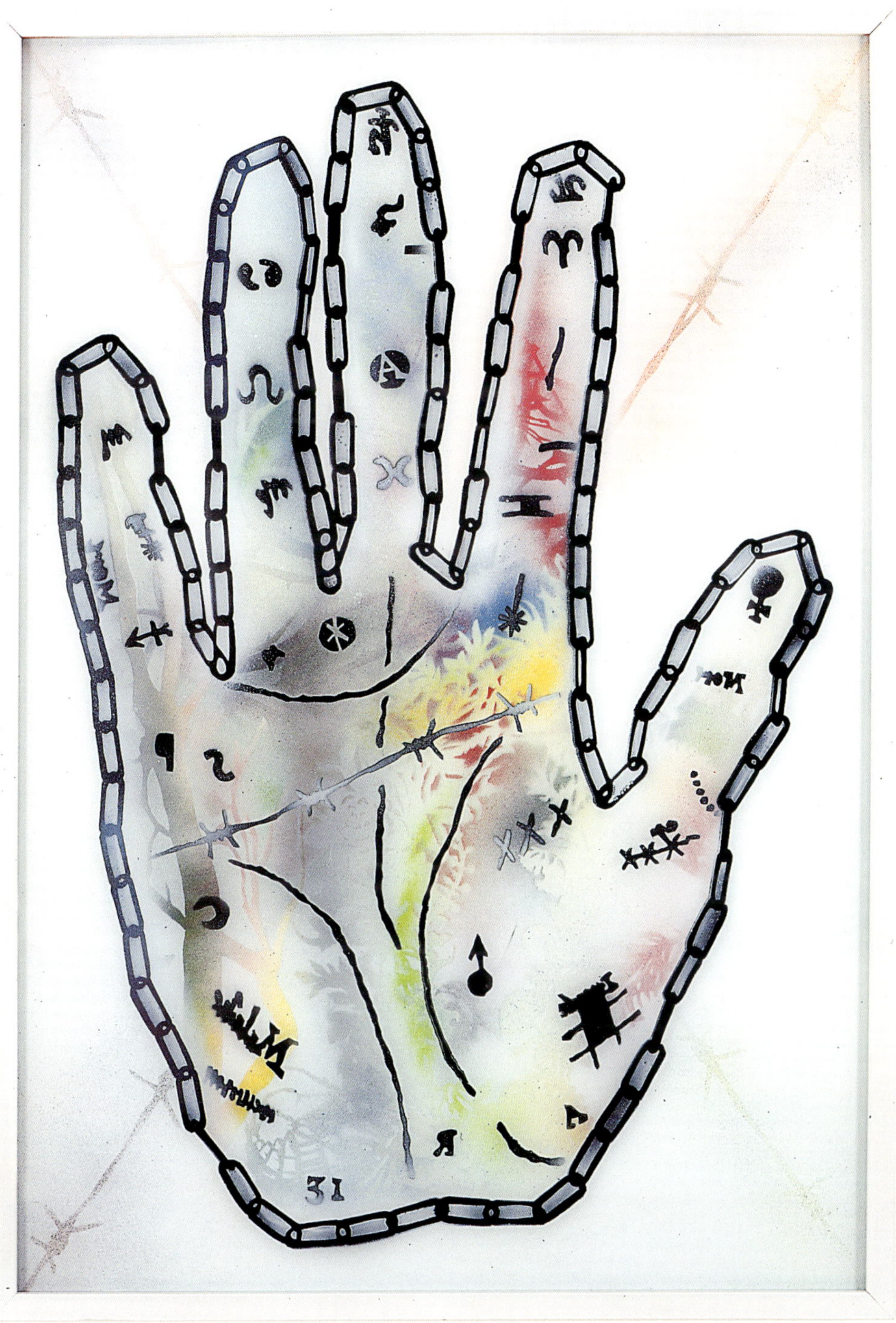

Premonitions (Light), 2007, 103 × 73 cm

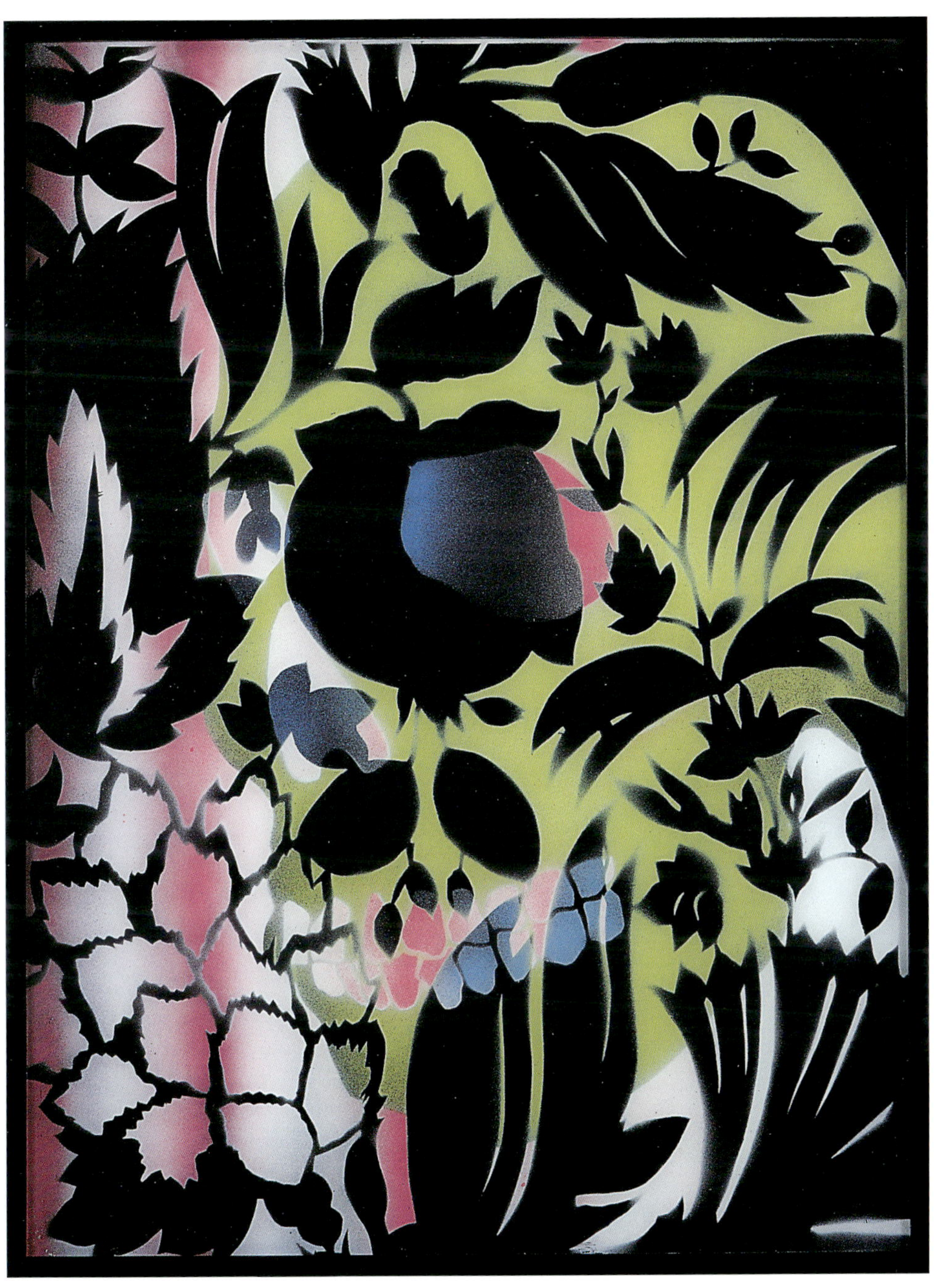

Remember Nothing, 2007, 82 × 62 cm

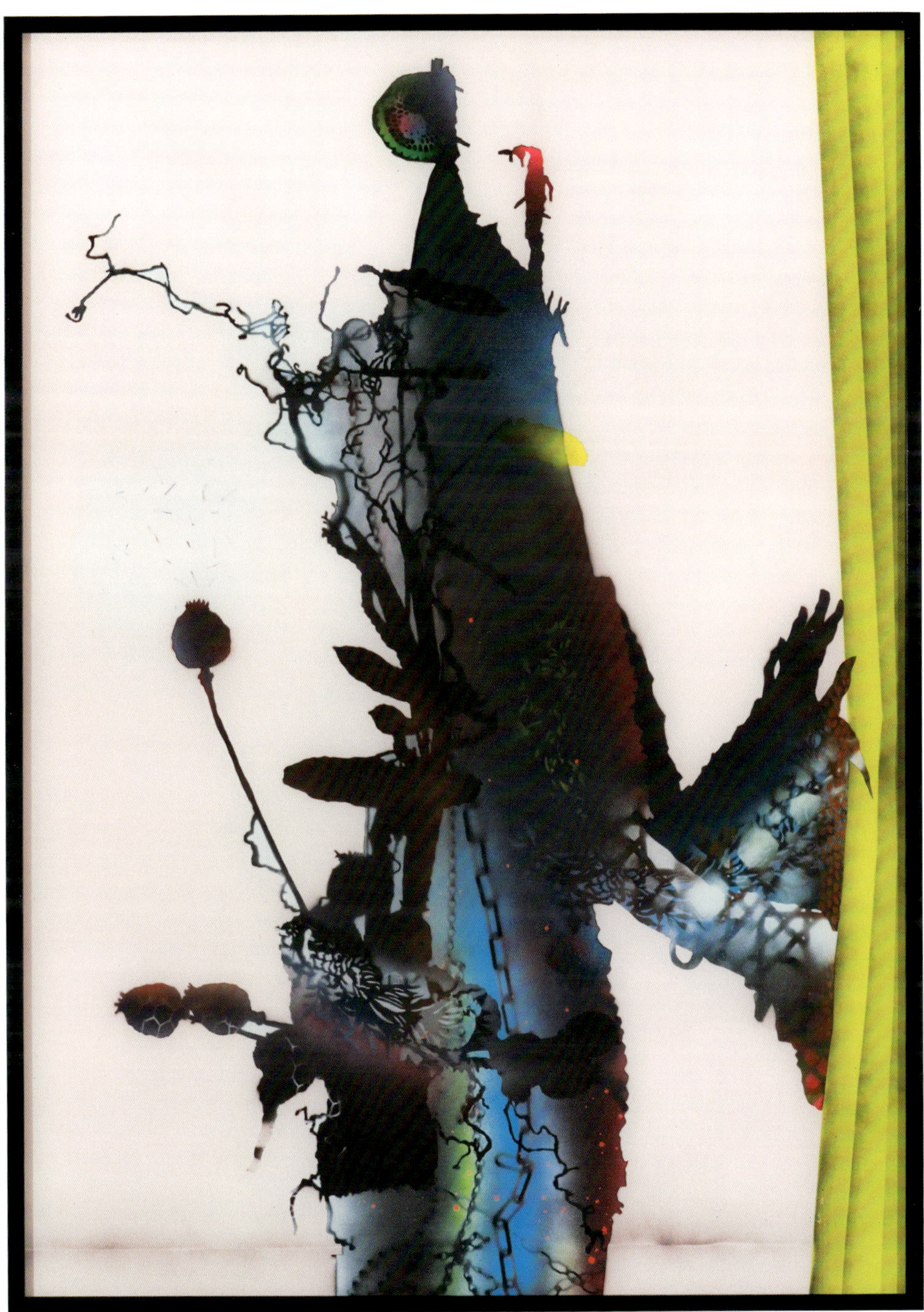

Neighbourhood Witch (yellow curtain), 2007, 163.5 × 118.5 cm

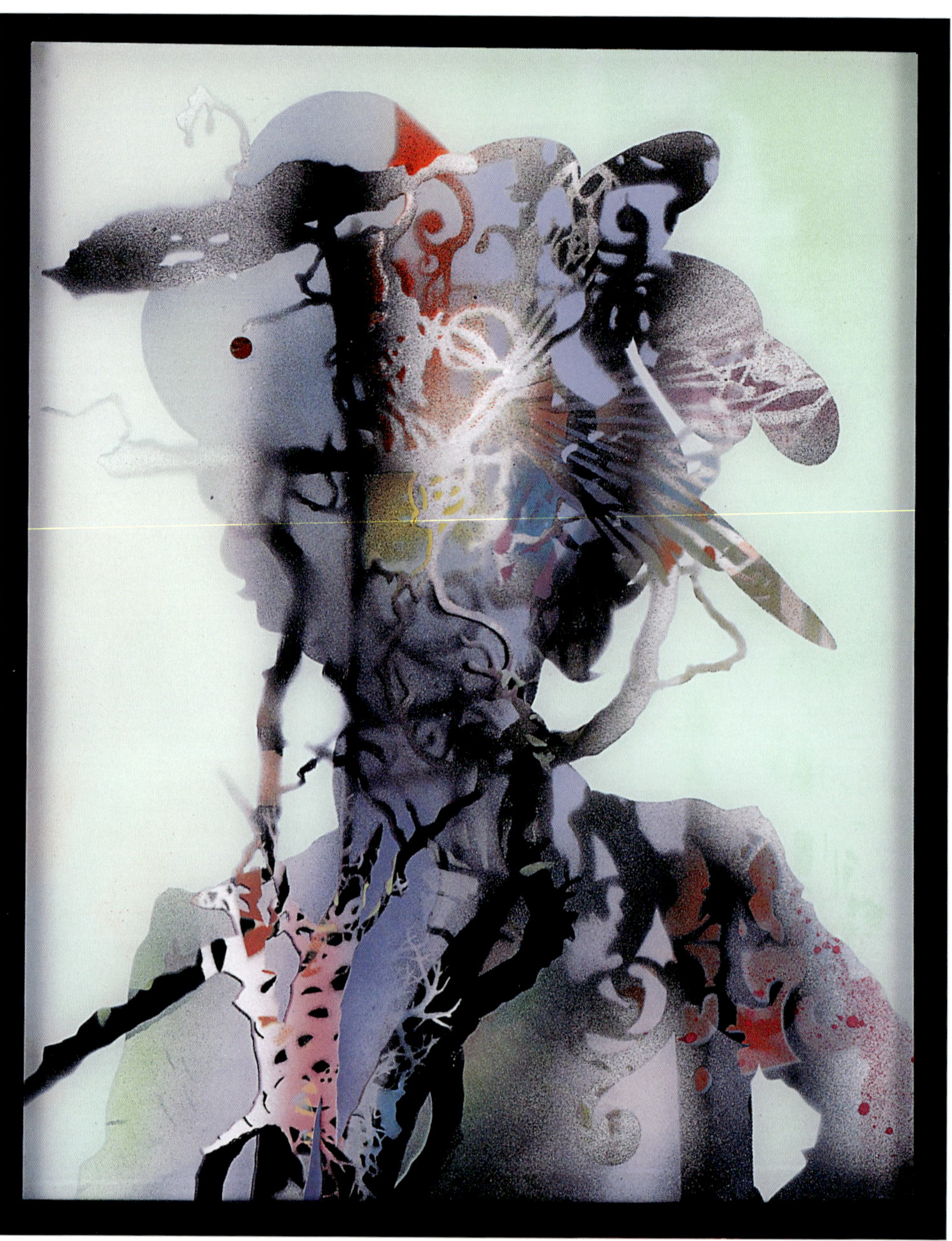

The Love Below, 2007, 52.2 × 42.1 cm

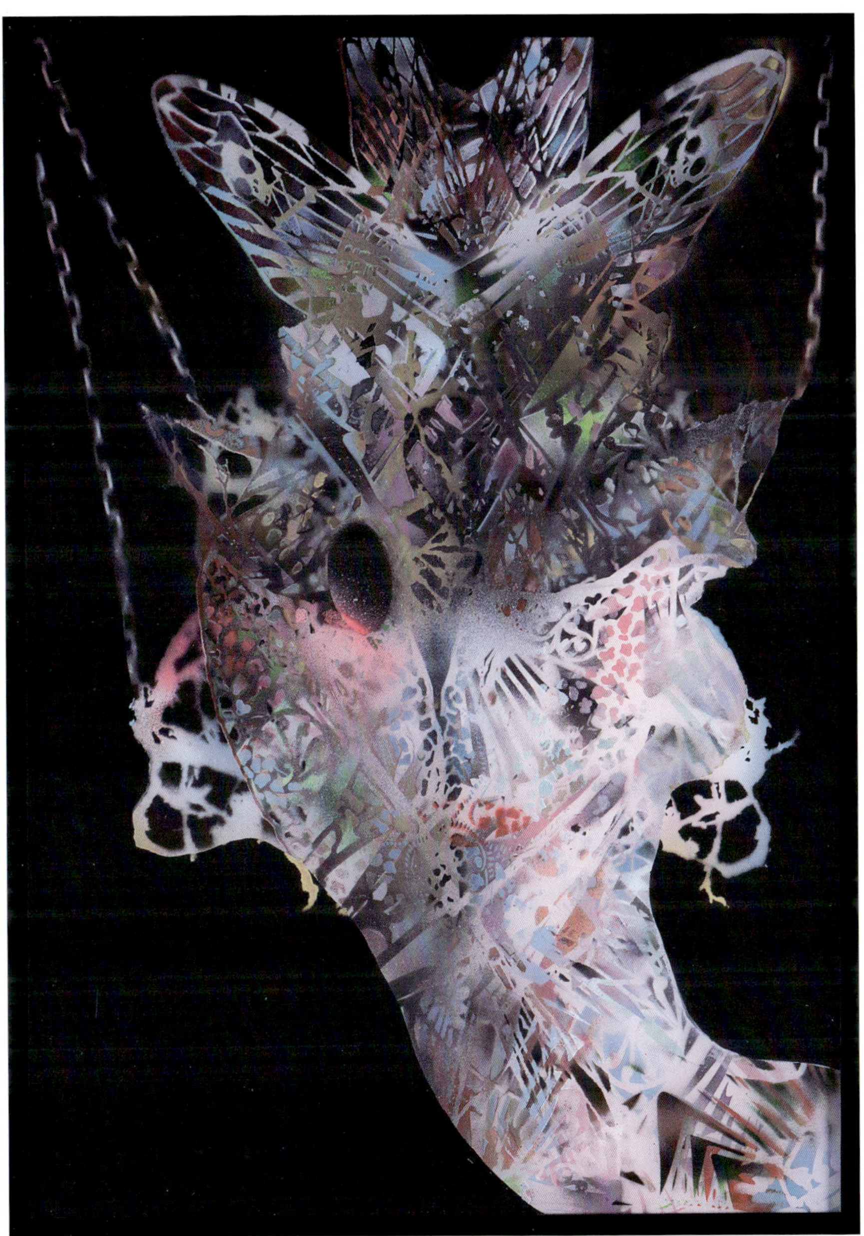

Cabbage White, 2008, 72.3 × 52.3 cm

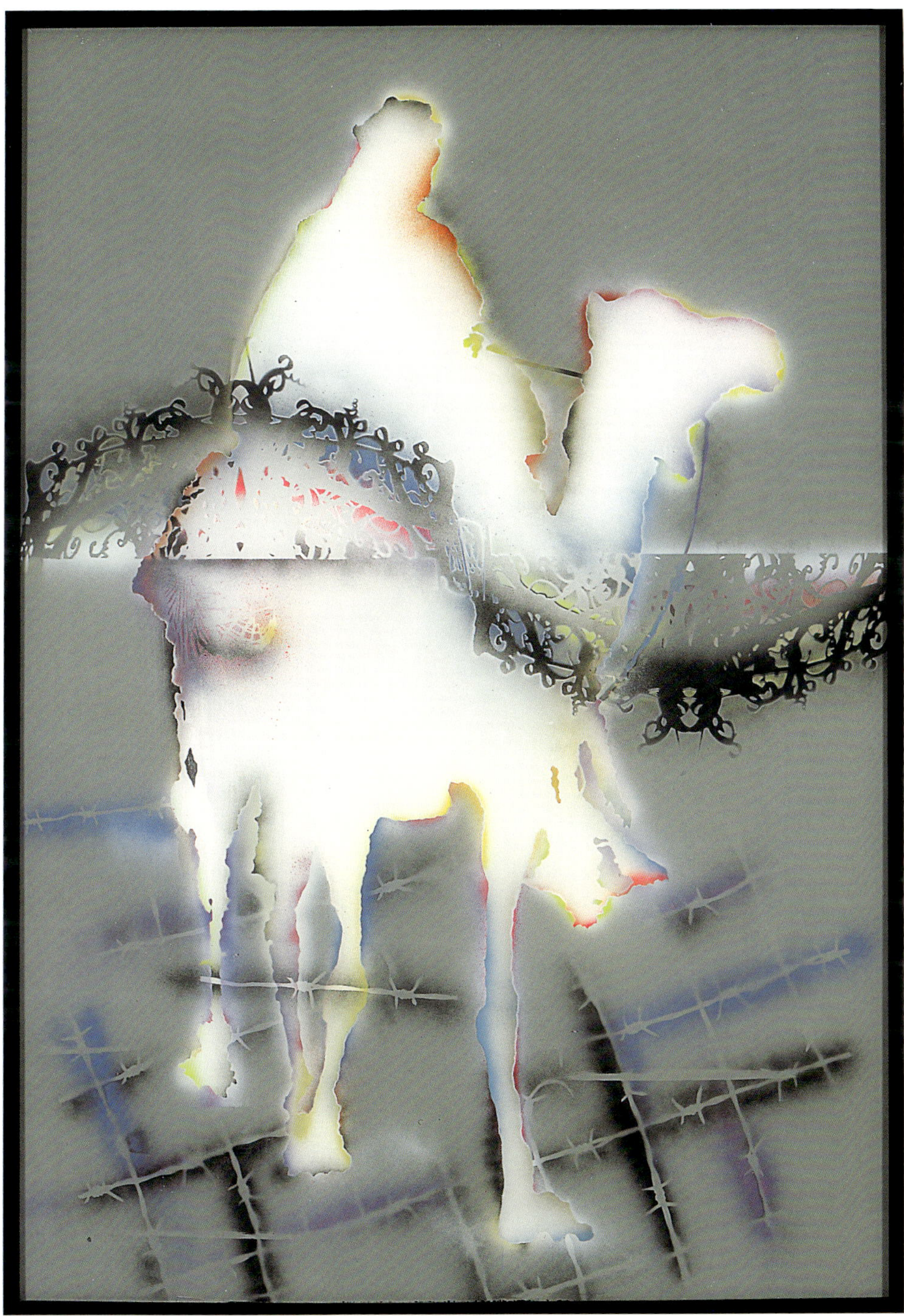

Ghost Train, 2007, 188.5 × 133.6 cm

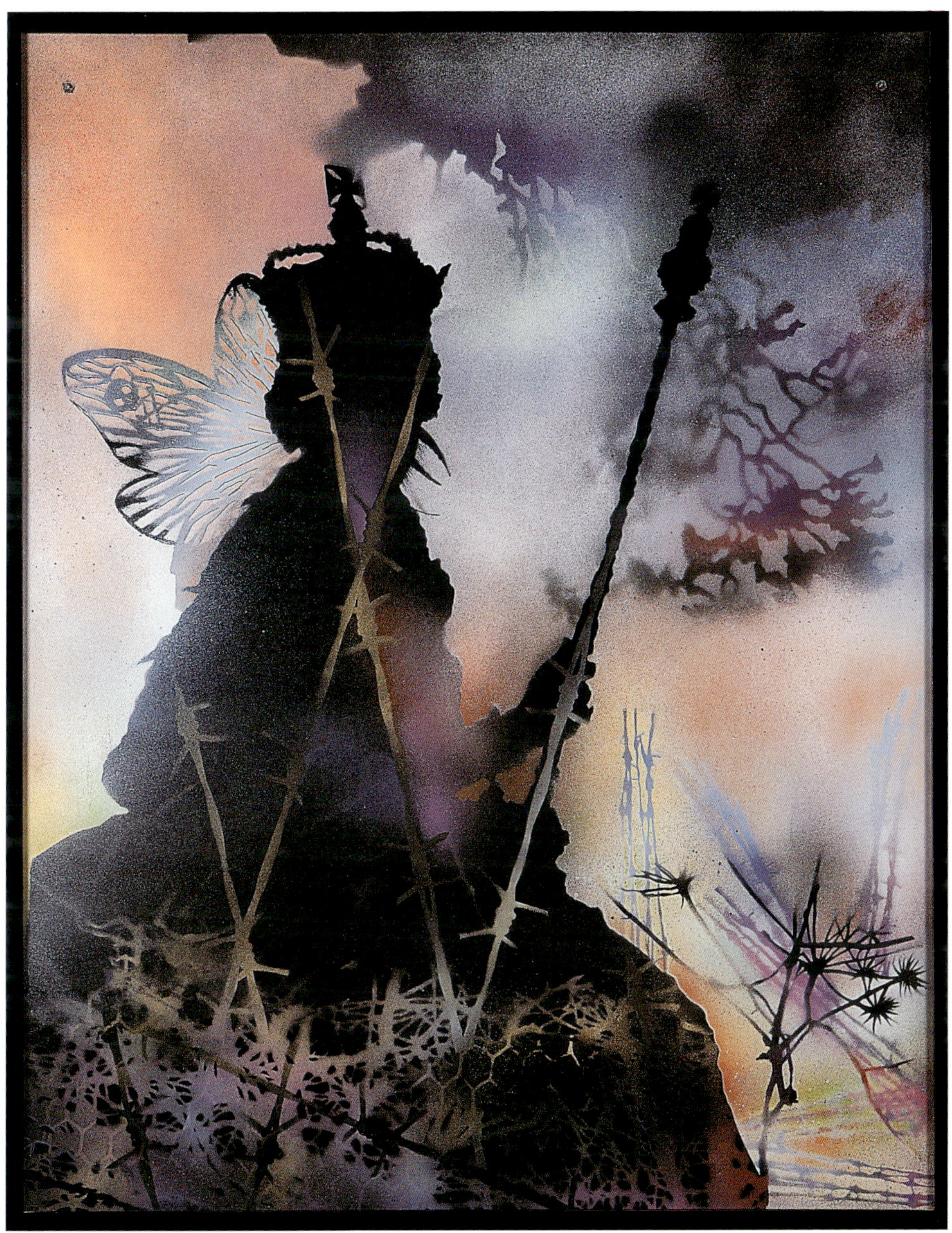

New Dawn Fades, 2007, 82 × 66 cm

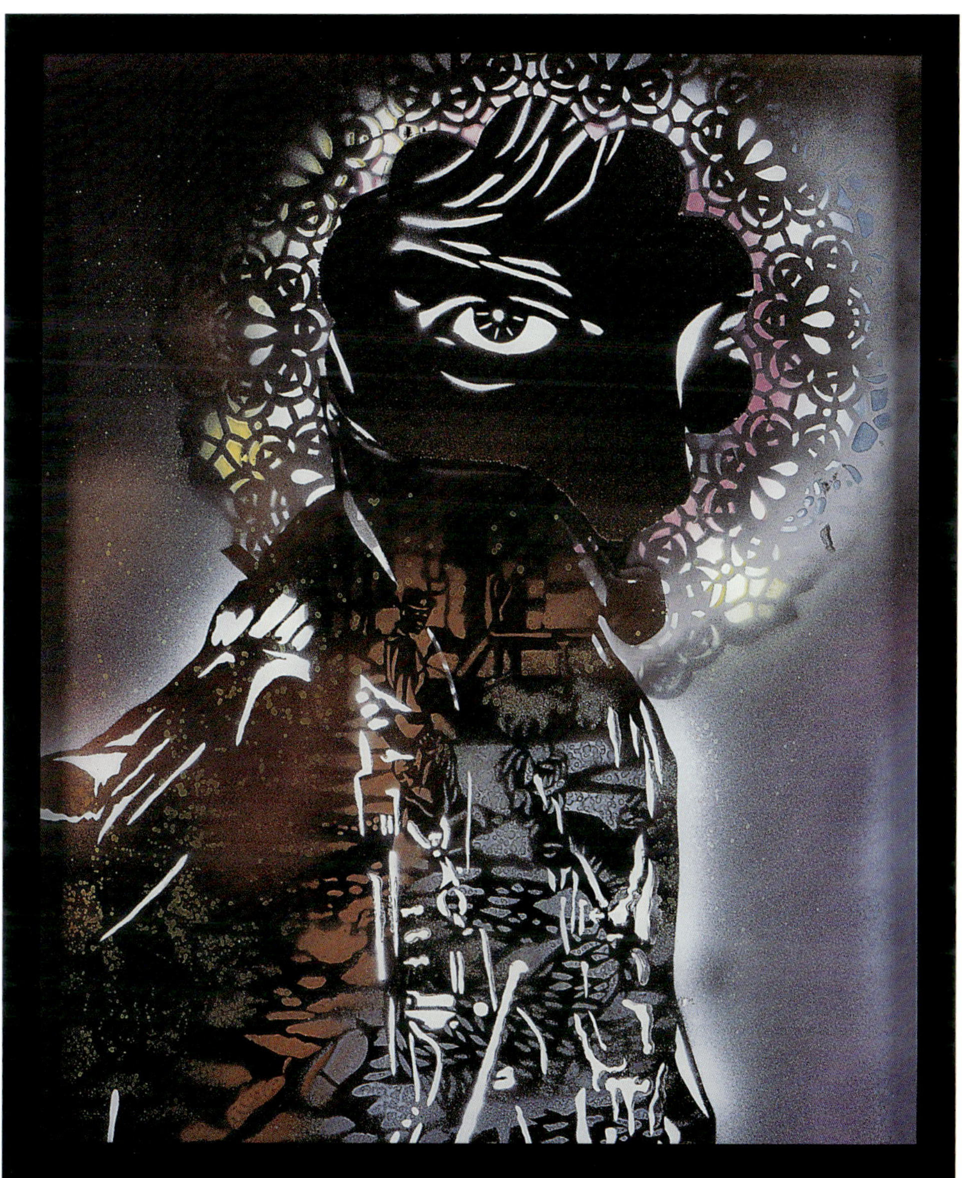

The Rider, 2006, 63 × 53 cm

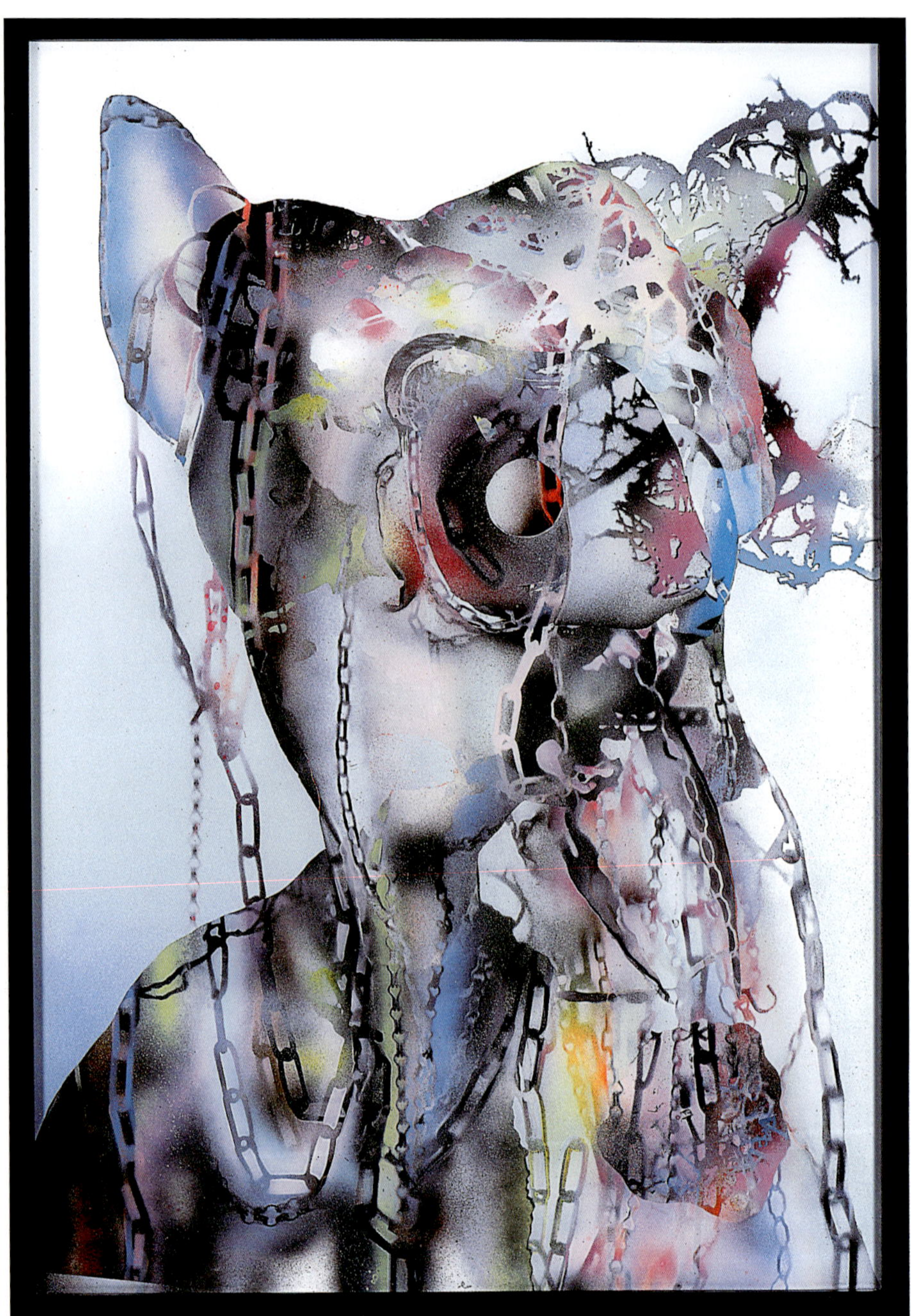

Gatekeeper, 2008, 103 × 73.5 cm

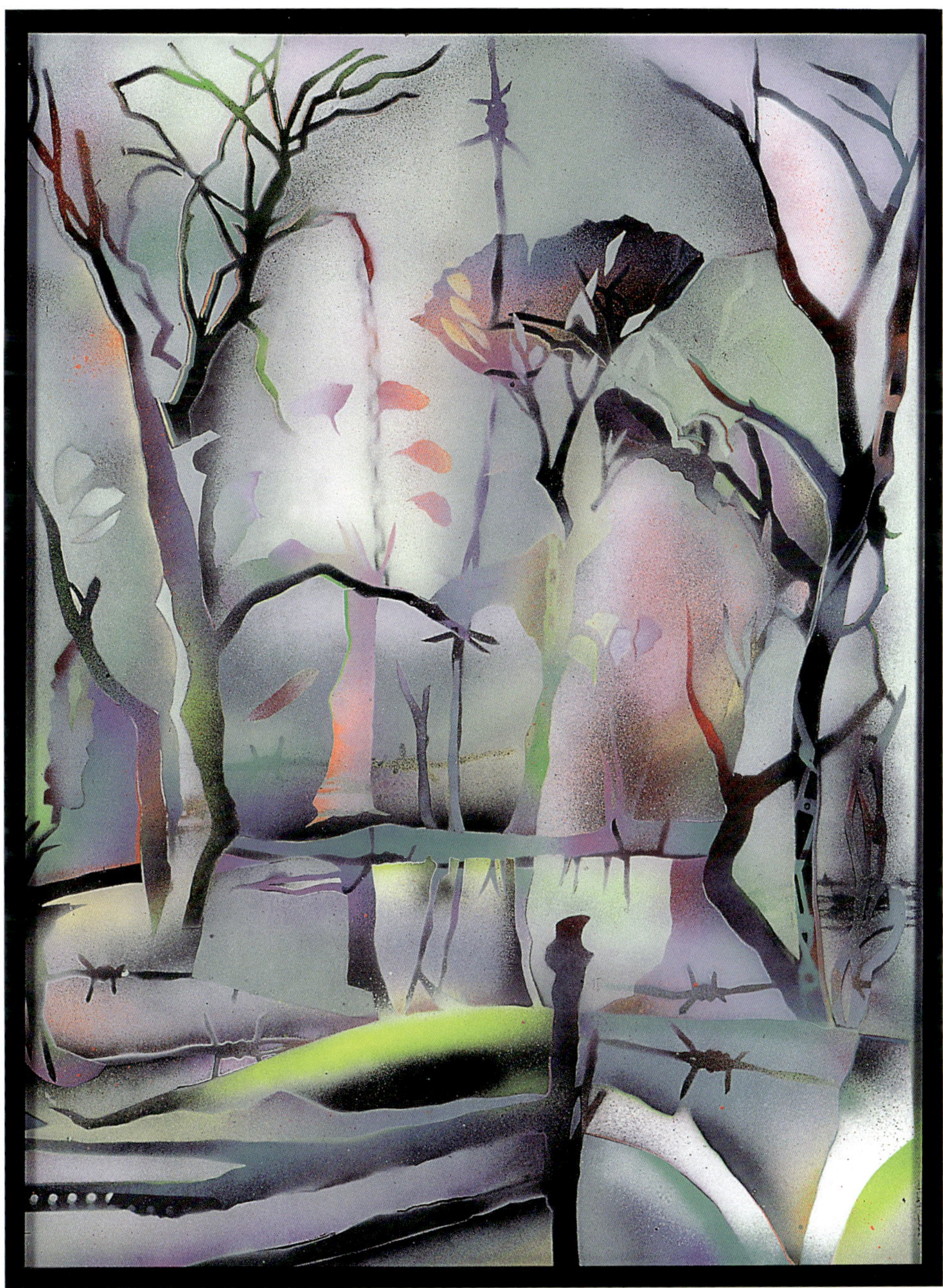

Sordid Sentimental, 2008, 82 × 62 cm

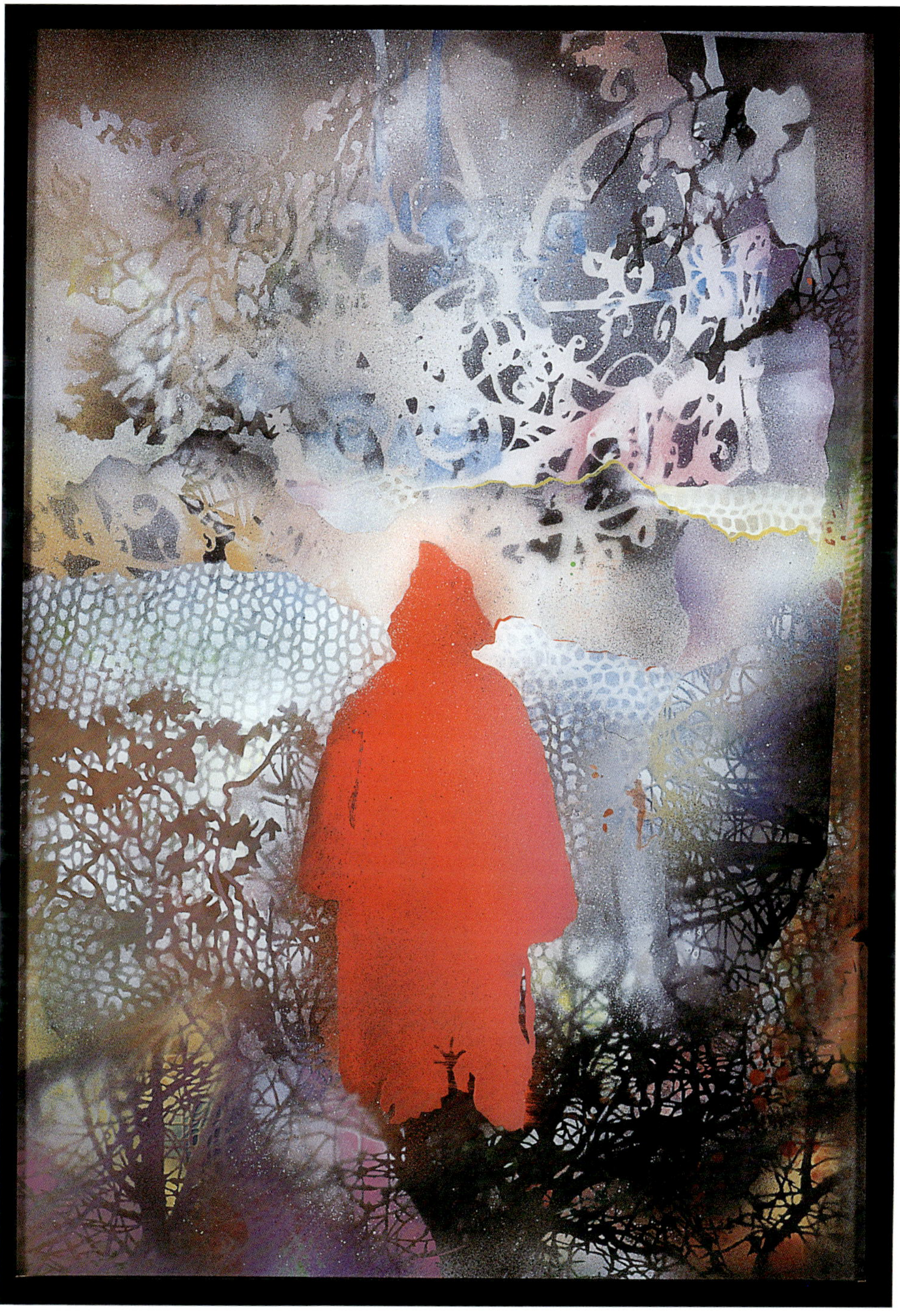

Back to Nature, 2007, 103 × 73 cm

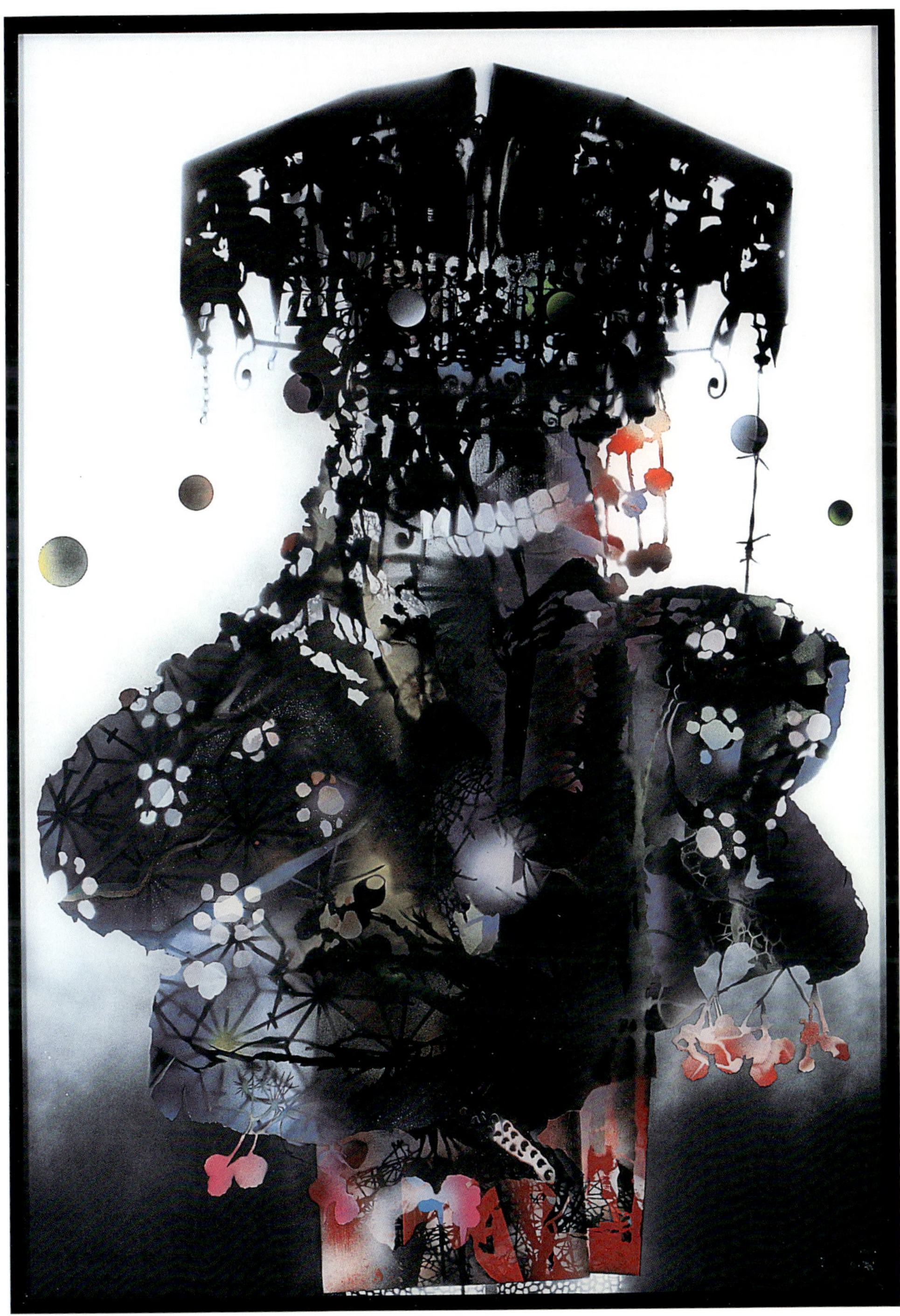

Civil War, 2007, 188.5 × 133.6 cm

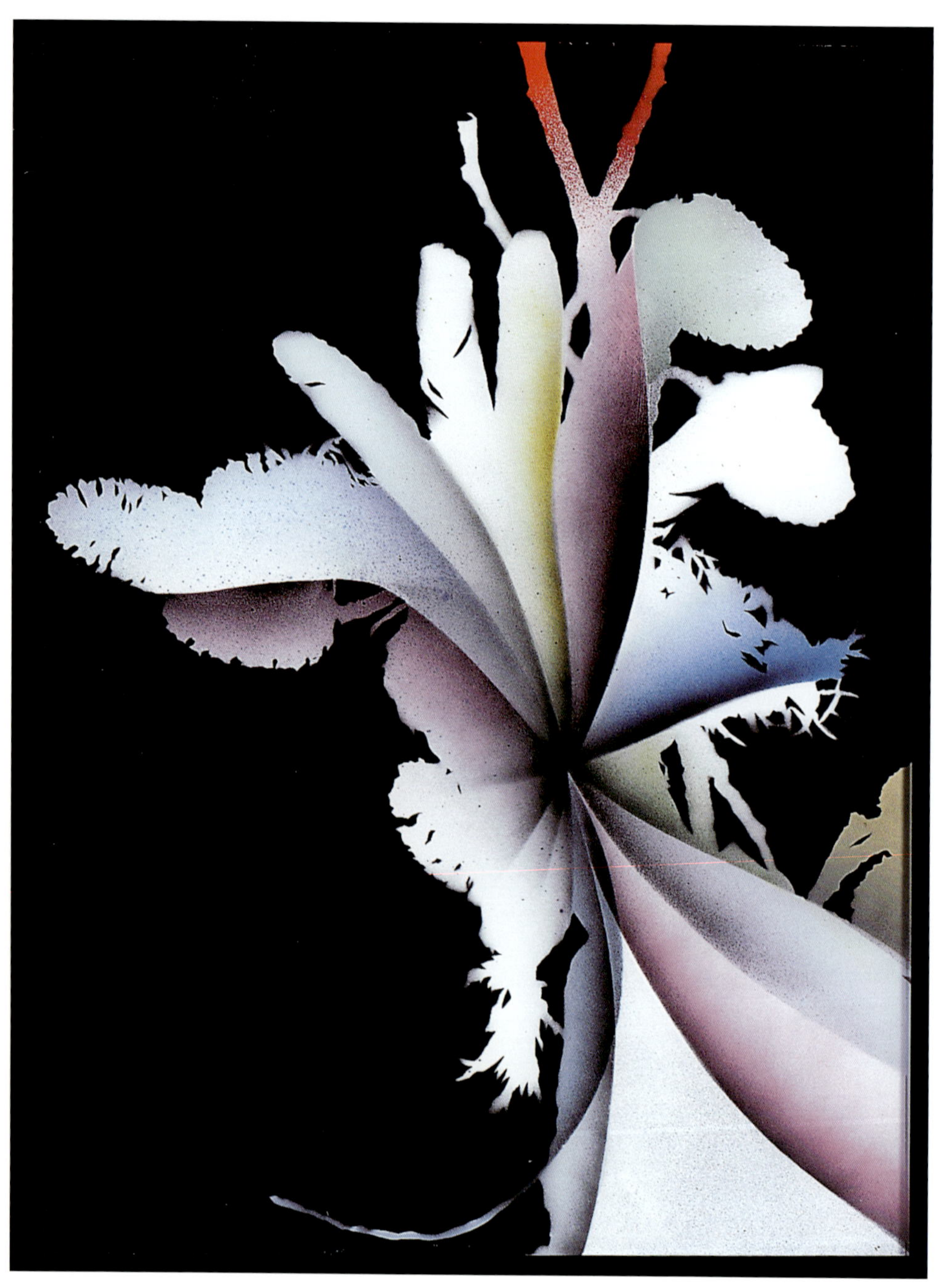

Flea Marketeer, 2008, 163.5 × 118.5 cm

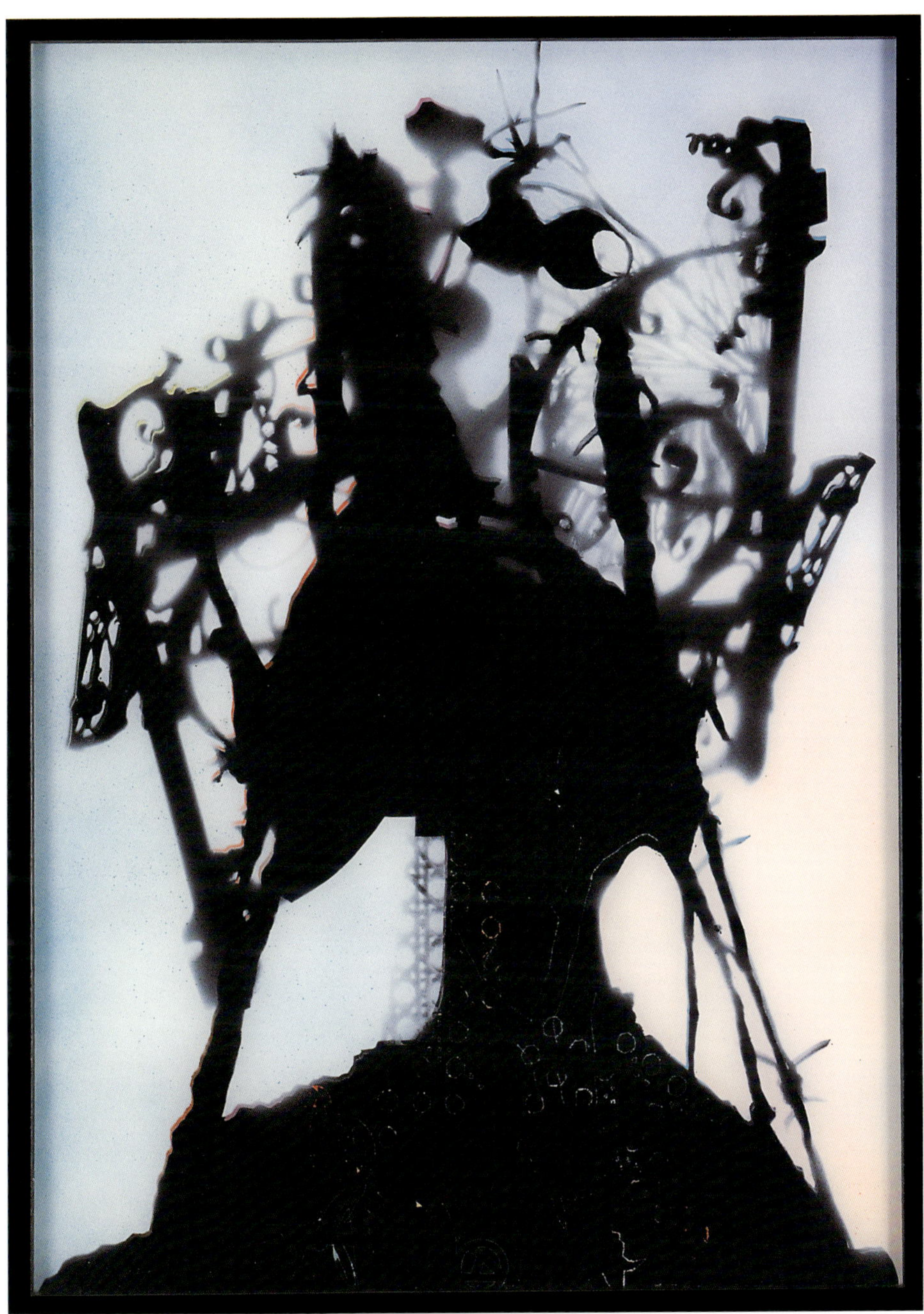

Hop Picker, 2007, 72.4 × 52.5 cm

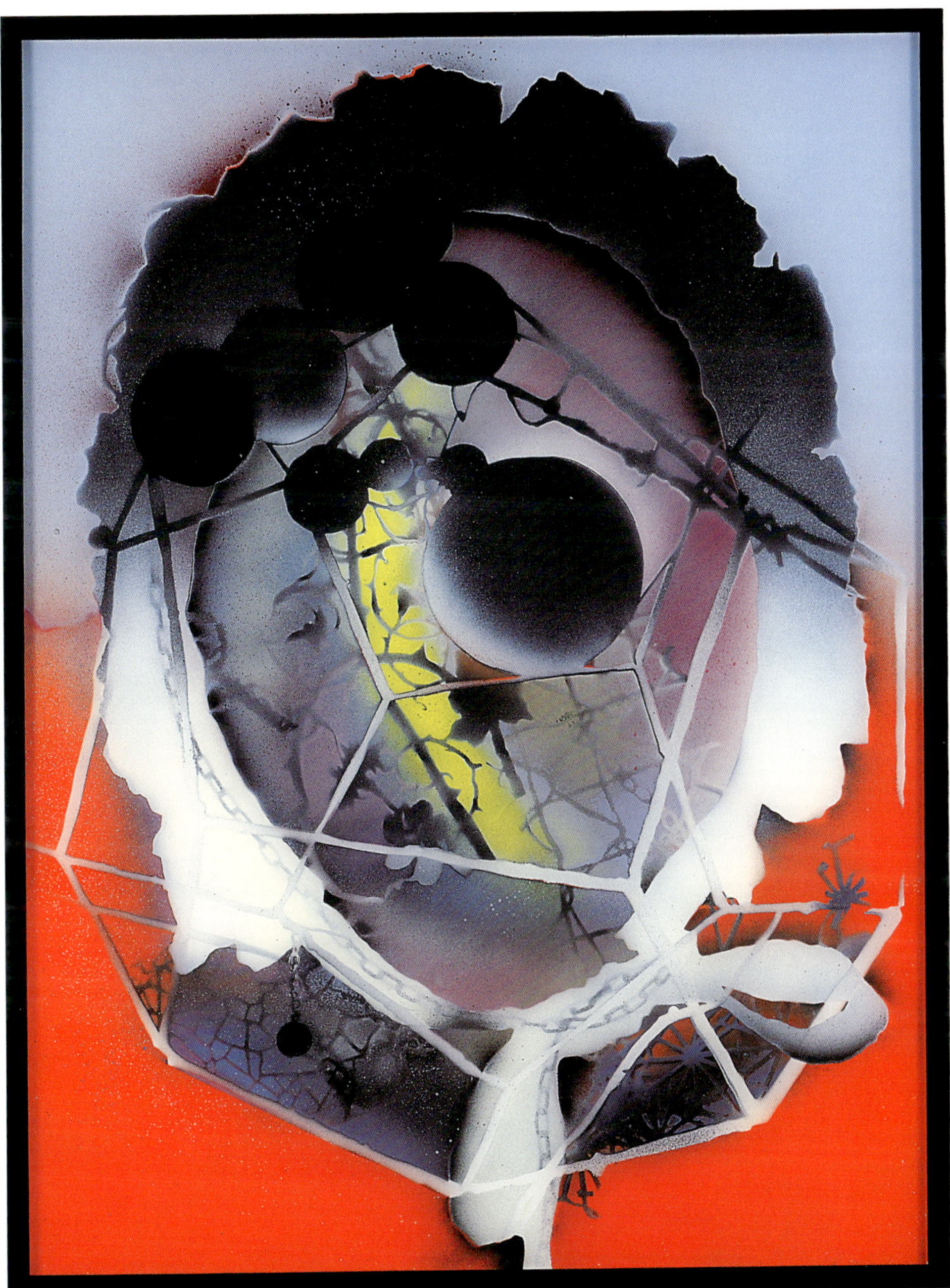

Red Admiral, 2008, 82.5 × 62.5 cm

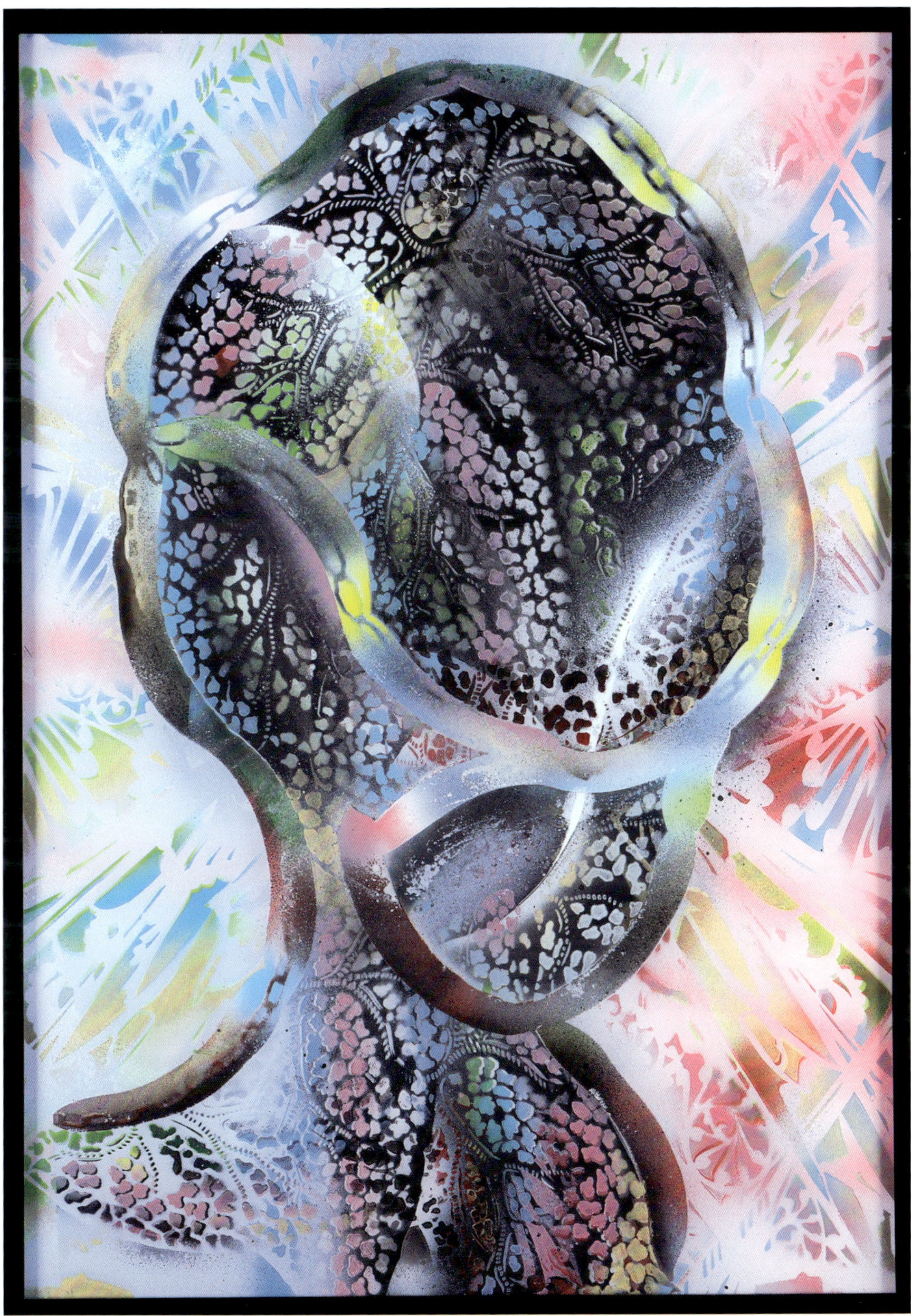

Painted Lady, 2008, 72.3 × 52.2 cm

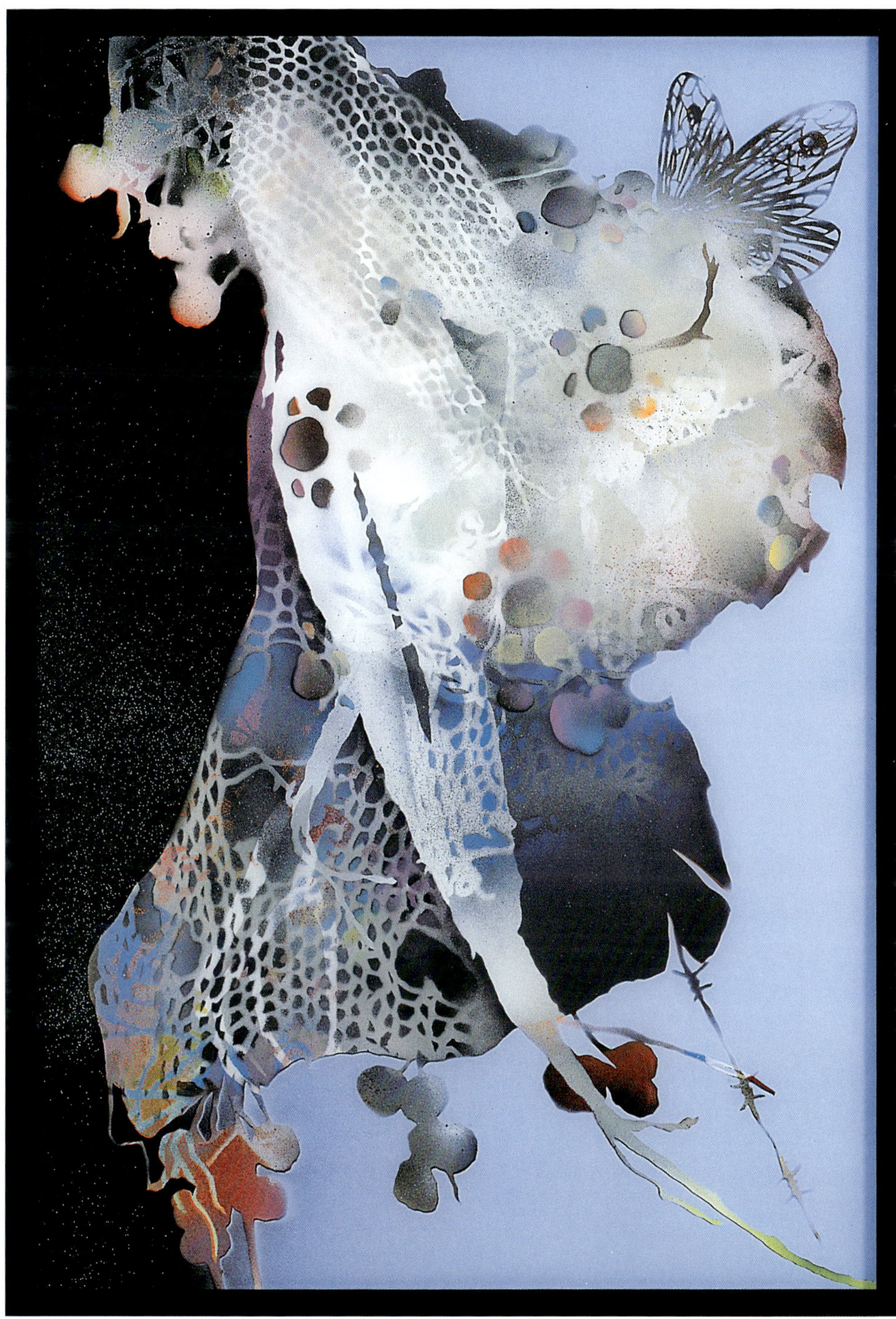

Stealer, 2007, 103 × 73 cm

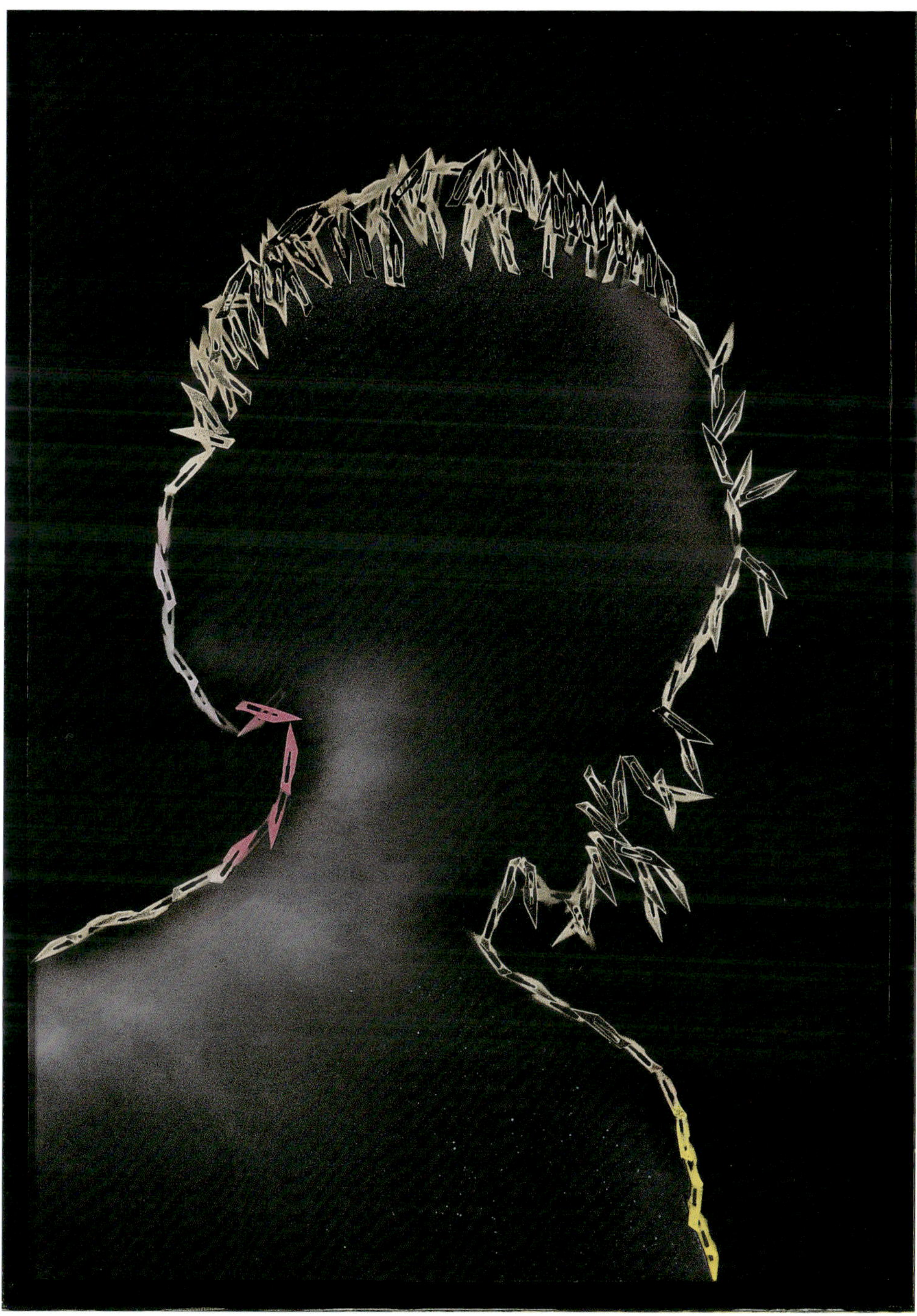

The Operator, 2007, 72.4 × 52 cm

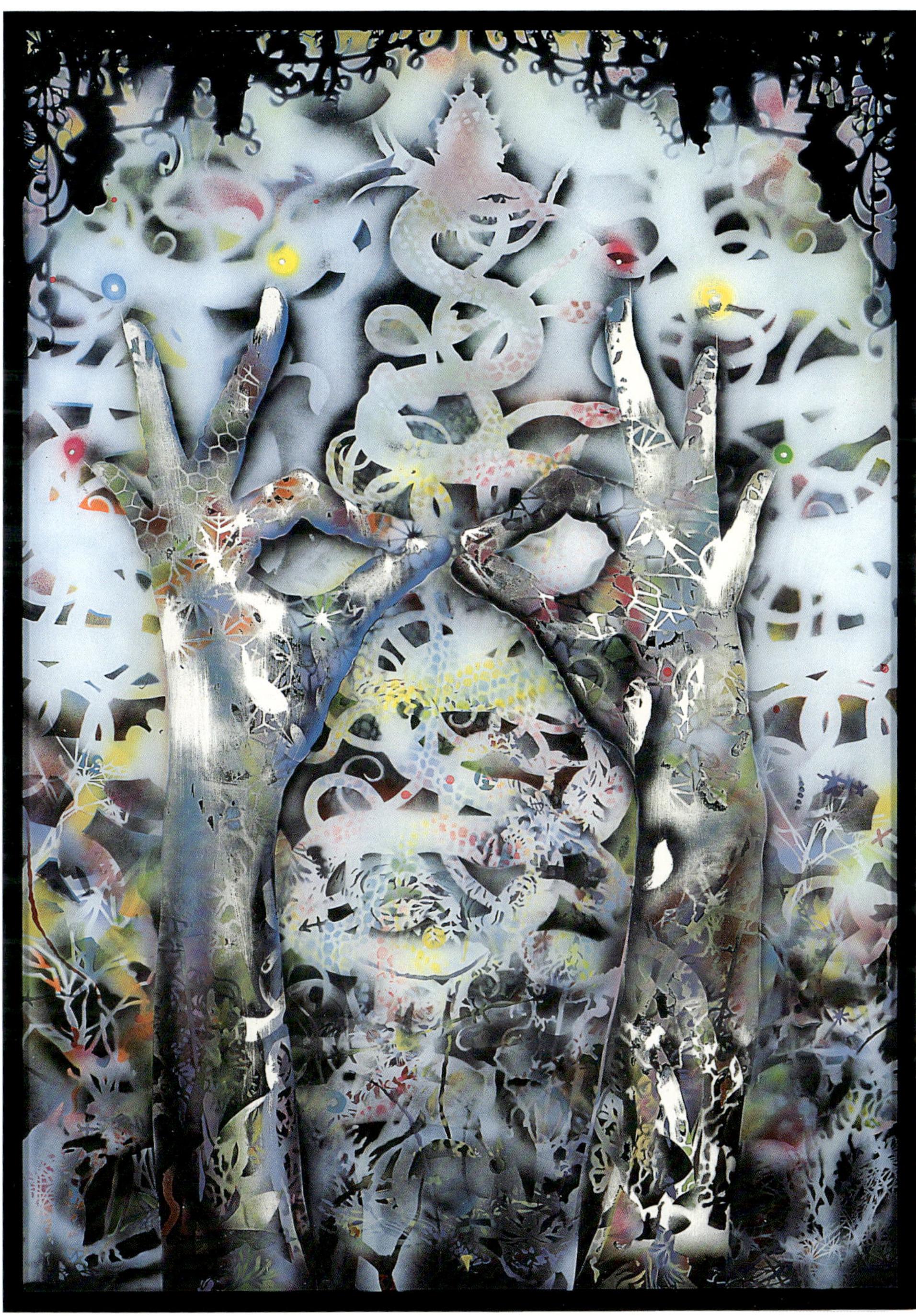

The Charmer, 2007, 163.5 × 118.5 cm

Biography

1964
Born in England

1986–90
Central Saint Martins School of Art,
London

Solo Exhibitions
2008
A Rabble of Butterflies, galerist, Istanbul

2007
Back to Nature, Sadie Coles HQ, London
Sordid Sentimental, Vacío 9, Madrid
Simon Periton, The Modern Institute,
Glasgow

2005
Peartree Farm, Peter Pears Gallery,
Aldeburgh, Suffolk
The Penis Mightier than the Sword, Karyn
Lovegrove Gallery, Los Angeles

2004
The Edge of the World, Sadie Coles HQ,
London
Ragamuffin, Vacío 9, Madrid
Street, Changing Role Gallery, Naples

2003
Mint Poisoner, Inverleith House, Royal
Botanic Garden Edinburgh
Snip Riot Omen, The Modern Institute,
Glasgow
Premonitions, Gorney Bravin + Lee,
New York

Flag, Gallery 4, Henry Moore Gallery,
Leeds

2002
Simon Periton, Karyn Lovegrove Gallery,
Los Angeles

2001
Simon Periton, galerist, Istanbul
Simon Periton, Jablonka Galerie, Linn
Lühn, Cologne
Cold warmed up, Sadie Coles HQ, London

2000
Simon Periton, Karyn Lovegrove Gallery,
Los Angeles
Simon Periton, Statements Booth,
Art Basel

1999
Barroquade, Simon Periton, foyer project
at the Hayward Gallery, London

1998
Simon Periton, Camden Arts Centre,
London

1997
Habitat (with David Thorpe), Kings
Road, London
Dandeliceum, Sadie Coles HQ, London
Simon Periton, Skinner's Cage, London
Simon Periton, British Council Window
Gallery, Prague

1994
Strange Spectacle (with Alan Kane),
Gallerie 217, Sportsverbande, Frankfurt
am Main

1993

Gild the Lily (with Alan Kane), E1, London
Weekender (with Alan Kane), Caledonia
Street, London

1992

Simon Periton, Bipasha Ghosh, London

1991

Seeds of Hope (with Georgie Hopton),
Wilson Hale, London
Olde World (with Georgie Hopton),
The Caraway Installation, Butlers Wharf,
London
Hope Project (with Georgie Hopton),
Frieze, London

Public Commissions
2008

Commissioned artist for
firstsite:newsite public gallery, opening
2009 in Colchester, England

2007

The Anti Room of the Mae Queen,
commission for new entrance to the
Victoria and Albert Museum, London

2006

French Letter, commissioned by Vamp
for UBS launch in the Turbine Hall,
Tate Modern, London
Future Punk, Selfridges, London

2005

Haberdasher, commission for the British
Home Office building of the Deputy
High Commission, Chennai, India

2004

Banner, temporary commission for
opening of BBC Media Centre, Wood
Lane, London
Strange Attractor, commission for London
Headquarters of Channel 4 Television,
London

2003

Vol-au-Vent, permanent sculptural
commission, British Airways
Headquarters, Heathrow Airport,
London

2002

Hole, window design for British Council
building in Brussels
Free Radicals, façade light projection,
commission for the 150th Anniversary of
the Victoria and Albert Museum, London